Restoring Trust in American Business

American Academy of Arts and Sciences

136 Irving Street
Cambridge, MA 02138-1996
Telephone: (617) 576-5000
Fax: (617) 576-5050
e-mail: aaas@amacad.org
Visit our Website at www.amacad.org

Restoring Trust in American Business

Edited by Jay W. Lorsch, Leslie Berlowitz, and Andy Zelleke

American Academy of Arts and Sciences
Cambridge, Massachusetts

The MIT Press
Cambridge, Massachusetts
London, England

MIT Press books may be purchased at special quantity discounts for business or sales promotional use. For information, please email special_sales@mitpress.mit.edu or write to Special Sales Department, The MIT Press, 5 Cambridge Center, Cambridge, MA 02142.

This book was set in Galliard by Anne Read.
Printed and bound in the United States of America.

Library of Congress Cataloging-in-Publication Data

Restoring trust in American business / edited by Jay W. Lorsch, Leslie Berlowitz, and Andy Zelleke.
    p.   cm.
  Includes bibliographical references and index.
  ISBN: 0-262-24048-3 (hc.:alk. paper)–0-262-74027-3 (pbk.:alk. paper)
  1. Corporate governance—United States. 2. Social responsibility of business—United States. I. Lorsch, Jay William. II. Berlowitz, Leslie. III. Zelleke, Andy.

HD2741.R475 2005
658.4'08 22—dc22

2004058358

10 9 8 7 6 5 4 3 2

Contents

Introduction

LESLIE BERLOWITZ AND ANDY ZELLEKE

As John Reed observes in this volume, "All is not well in corporate America....We have severely harmed the trust and confidence essential to free market capitalism." There is no question but that the recent wave of corporate scandals has eroded confidence in the American business community. A complex of safeguards relied upon to check managerial wrongdoing failed. This volume examines the causes of this failure, considers ways to guard against such breakdowns in the future, and proposes directions for restoring trust in American business.

The American Academy has had a long-standing interest in the success and stability of America's economic institutions, including the business firm. From the 1781 report that charged the Fellows to "attend to the subject of the Commerce of America" to the 1988 study *The U.S. Business Corporation: An Institution in Transition,* the Academy has seen a healthy business environment as an indispensable component of national stability.[1]

The Enron and WorldCom scandals spawned a series of welcome inquiries and legislative actions. At the same time, three leaders in the world of American business—corporate lawyers Martin Lipton and Larry Sonsini and management scholar Jay Lorsch—launched a longer-term Academy study by scholars and practitioners. As a first step, they convened a group of leaders from law, journalism, government, investment banking, corporate governance, management, and a variety of scholarly disciplines to examine the roots of the problems facing American

---

[1] John R. Meyer and James M. Gustafson, eds., *The U.S. Business Corporation: An Institution in Transition* (Cambridge, MA: American Academy of Arts and Sciences, 1988).

business and to recommend a long-term course of action. This book is the initial result of the group's work.

It is clear that corporate management has, on too many occasions, ignored even its legally mandated fiduciary obligations. Why have respected business firms so egregiously failed the public's relatively modest expectation that companies "play by the rules" and follow the law? This volume highlights the vital role that a mix of private and public sector "gatekeepers"—members of traditional professions, such as lawyers and accountants, as well as corporate directors, regulators, investment bankers, and business journalists—are expected to play in our economy.

The three papers in Part I provide historical perspectives on the broader corporate system, on business culture, and on professionalism. Mark Roe's paper suggests that two basic sources of instability in the American corporate governance system have been at the root of its recurring problems: large business firms are rarely managed by their owners; and the regulatory framework for business is both fragmented and porous. These structural features entail costs and risks as well as benefits; and Roe argues that as a society the best we can do is manage—but never eliminate—the inherent vulnerabilities.

John Reed's paper outlines seminal changes in American business over the past several decades. He observes that "The cult of stockholder value has been corrupting," and suggests that a breakdown in personal values is at the root of the recent business scandals. In proposing reforms for corporate boards and for the financial services industry, he emphasizes that our capitalist system ultimately depends on maintaining individual values. The paper by Rakesh Khurana, Nitin Nohria, and Daniel Penrice outlines the criteria for professionalism and applies these criteria to corporate executives. It argues provocatively that a transformation of management into a bona fide profession would be a salutary development.

Each of the papers in Part II explores a single gatekeeper role. While the essays on auditors and lawyers examine the parameters of two of our society's most well-established professions, the other essays in this section deal with occupations that our society has yet to recognize as full-fledged professions. The common thread of this latter group of essays is the argument that responsible corporate conduct would likely be advanced if the practitioners of all these occupations were to develop self-conscious professional identities.

Donald Langevoort discusses the regulator role, focusing on the federal securities regulators at the Securities and Exchange Commission. While the very *raison d'être* of the SEC is to serve the public interest, Langevoort acknowledges the need, after the past decade, for "restoring within the agency a professional culture that...attracts people with a deep commitment to its mission."

Martin Lipton and Jay Lorsch argue the merits of professionalizing the corporate directorship. In their view, professionalization would entail refocusing directors on the long-term success of their companies, and "indoctrinating them into a common code of conduct" with clearer goals. Margaret Blair applauds the Lipton and Lorsch proposal, but also notes that director professionalization is unlikely to dislodge the "short-term share value maximization" obsession that has been ascendant for more than a decade.

Damon Silvers asserts that there is a deficit in meaningful accountability in the boardroom that can only be rectified by empowering long-term institutional shareholders vis-à-vis directors. Michael Klausner emphasizes the limits of corporate law as a lever for improving board governance, but sees potential promise in the deliberate fostering of professional director norms advocated by Lipton and Lorsch.

William Kinney acknowledges the professional gatekeeper role of auditors, but cautions that the public's expectations as to the nature and scope of that role have exceeded what these professionals can plausibly deliver. This expectations gap is part of the current crisis facing the accounting profession and threatens that profession's ability to emerge from the shadows of the corporate scandals. John Biggs endorses Kinney's efforts to focus auditor attention—and the public's expectations—primarily on the prevention of financial reporting fraud.

William Allen and Geoffrey Miller contend that the legal profession has evolved in recent decades from a "club" to a "market" model. This change has gravely weakened the commitment of business lawyers to the "discernible spirit" of the law—as opposed to their commitment to zealous advocacy on behalf of paying clients. This reduced commitment to the law helps explain the complicity of lawyers in some of the recent scandals. Richard Painter cautions that the "club" model proved, historically, to have its own grave infirmities. He concludes that self-regulation is unlikely to keep lawyers—or, for that matter, members of other professions—from harming those outside the club.

Felix Rohatyn documents the massive transformation of investment banking into an industry that has distanced bankers from their traditional function of offering "advice to corporations and protection to investors." In this sense, even though the investment banker role has never been one that would meet Khurana, Nohria, and Penrice's criteria for a bona fide profession, it was once far more profession-like than it is today. Gerald Rosenfeld observes that "When an investment banker can earn a lifetime's worth of compensation—or ten lifetimes' worth—in one or two years of extreme markets, the pressure on behavior is sometimes too great to bear." He therefore proposes that the industry consider taking steps to become a fully self-conscious profession with explicit values and norms of conduct.

While journalism is regarded by many as having elements of a profession, Geneva Overholser details the growing challenges to professionalism among business journalists in particular. She proposes that the quality of business reporting can and should be improved. She also cautions that media organizations are, increasingly, large corporations subject to their own market pressures that are in tension with the highest professional standards.

These essays are followed by the Report of the Academy's Corporate Responsibility Steering Committee. It includes a set of "Recommendations for Practice" designed to enhance gatekeeper professionalism.

The Corporate Responsibility project is a work in progress. As Mark Roe suggests, the interdependent parts of the corporate governance system will continually need balancing and rebalancing. Maintaining trust—and trustworthiness—in business is a challenge calling for long-term vigilance, not a task to be completed once and forgotten. In that spirit, this volume's essays and recommendations are intended to help stimulate an important conversation about professionalism in American business.

* * *

The Academy is deeply grateful to Steering Committee co-chairs Martin Lipton, Jay Lorsch, and Larry Sonsini. This volume grew out of their initiative and strong leadership. We are also grateful to the other members of the Steering Committee who helped shape both the project and this book: William Allen, John Biggs, Margaret Blair, Richard Buxbaum, Alfred Chandler, James Cochrane, Michael Gellert, Amory Houghton, Jr., Rakesh Khurana, Douglass North, Geneva Overholser, John S. Reed, Mark Roe, Felix Rohatyn, Gerald Rosenfeld, John Rosenwald, Damon Silvers, and Michael Useem.

Special thanks to Senator Paul Sarbanes, who shared his perspective with members of the Steering Committee; to John S. Reed, whose paper was the focus of a workshop held at the House of the Academy in April 2003; and to the other authors of this volume's other essays, many of which were initially drafted for workshops in collaboration with the New York University Center for Law & Business. Thanks are also due to panelists Mark Carter, Michael Cook, Conrad Harper, Samuel Hayes, Steven Lipin, Kenneth Roman, Walter Shipley, and Leo Strine.

Our appreciation goes to the other individuals who participated in project workshops and discussions, including Alex D'Arbeloff, Jennifer Arlen, Michael Barnett, Francis Bator, Lucian Bebchuk, James Block, Joan Bok, John Brademas, Charles Brock, Louis Cabot, Lewis Cullman, Daniel Diamond, David Forney, Marion Fremont-Smith, Arthur Gelb, Stephen Gillers, William Golden, Robert Gordon, Charles Haar, George Lowy, Richard Meserve, Ashish Nanda, Peter Nicholas, Guy Nichols, Carl Pforzheimer, Thomas Phillips, Joshua Ronen, Richard Schmalensee, Muriel Siebert, Michael Sovern, Thomas Tyler, David Weinstein, and Bernard Yeung.

We would also like to recognize the indispensable contributions of members of the Academy's staff, especially Will Browder, who skillfully managed project logistics; Giffen Maupin, who continues to provide support; and Phyllis Bendell, whose expertise was invaluable in producing this volume. We are also grateful to John Covell of the MIT Press.

We gratefully acknowledge the support of the New York Stock Exchange Foundation, the Sloan Foundation and Georgetown Law Center, the New York University Center for Law & Business, and the Academy's Committee on Studies, as well as other generous donors for their contributions to the Academy's program fund.

PART I

Managers: Beyond Regulation

The Inevitable Instability of American Corporate Governance

MARK J. ROE

INTRODUCTION

The recent business crises seem new and different from what has gone on before. But at their core, they are not. The core fissure in American corporate governance is the separation of ownership from control—distant and diffuse stockholders, with concentrated management—a separation that creates both great efficiencies and recurring breakdowns. True, some of the Enron-class scandals' specific problems are new, or exaggerated forms of what's come before—special purpose vehicles with complex funding arrangements, unusually high executive compensation with stock options a dominating component, failure at a venerable accounting firm, some inattentive boards of directors—but the specifics still derive from the core structure of American corporate governance. We will solve the current issues—or, more plausibly, reduce them to manageable proportions—but then sometime later, somewhere else, another piece of the corporate apparatus will fail. We'll have another corporate governance crisis and it will emanate from the same basic source: that ownership has separated from control in large firms. We'll patch it up, we'll move on, we'll muddle through. That's what will happen this time, and that's what will happen next time.

Separation is the foundational instability of American corporate governance. But it's not the only key instability, and the current crises exemplify the other key one as well. We have a decentralized and porous regulatory system. Yes, decentralization has key advantages: regulatory specialization, multiple channels of information flowing into the regulators, and the potential for multiple regulatory players to loosely check one another, without an overarching, potentially rigid regulatory monolith. One regulator might miss the problem, but—we hope—another one catches it.

But decentralization's advantages come with two costs in porosity. And they're big ones. First off, a corporate crisis could arise in which no specialized regulator is immediately equipped to head off the problem; and each may think the task really belongs to another regulator, thought to be better equipped to handle the current problem.

Moreover, and probably more importantly, our decentralized regulatory system leaves each regulator with weaknesses; each has incomplete authority. And the regulated can, and often do, exploit these weaknesses, sometimes deterring the regulator from acting well, either by influencing political authorities to deny the regulator authority, or by fighting the potential regulations in courts and Congress. This porosity deters much over-regulation, an important advantage here. But it also can deter good regulation. The Enron-class scandals illustrate well this instability of American corporate governance: gatekeepers like accountants kept their regulatory climate weak and fought back regulatory attempts to reduce their conflicts of interest. The presumably regulated firms influenced the accounting measures of profitability, most famously in whether stock options paid to executives and employees should be expensed just like other employee pay. And in reaction to the corporate governance crises, the Securities and Exchange Commission is now considering tilting boardroom authority a little less strongly toward managers—although by no more than a few degrees—but in trying to do so, they've faced a buzz-saw of managerial opposition, opposition that has thus far stopped the SEC from recalibrating shareholder-managerial authority.

Combine these two instabilities and we can see a deeper structure to the Enron-class breakdowns. To mitigate the problems of separation, markets and regulators have built institutions whose primary task is to check and validate managers' actions, since the separation of ownership from control raises the risk of managerial misdeeds. Some of that checking—"gatekeeping," in corporate governance parlance—is itself regulated. But with our porous system of regulation, the core regulated group—the managers—can induce regulators to weaken the direct oversight that they face, can influence Congress to deny the regulators enough funding to be effective, can deter good regulation, and can thereby render some gatekeepers ineffectual in checking managers. There's more than a little of that combination—a one-two punch to the belly of American corporate governance—in the Enron group of scandals.

▶ With our porous system of regulation, the core regulated group—the managers—can induce regulators to weaken the direct oversight that they face, can influence Congress to deny the regulators enough funding to be effective, can deter good regulation, and can thereby render some gatekeepers ineffectual in checking managers.

I. THE FUNDAMENTAL FISSURE

A. The Concept

By the end of the nineteenth century, the engineering advances in a continent-wide economy made large-scale production efficient. With the railroads running across the nation, production could be huge and local, but distribution could be national.[1] The capital needed for that kind of production outstripped the capacity of even the wealthiest. To pool capital—especially in the cases of mergers and founders selling off their holdings—equity moved from controlling shareholders into dispersed stock markets, and ownership separated from control. The quintessential academic analysis came in Berle and Means' famous book.[2]

[1] Alfred D. Chandler, *The Visible Hand: The Managerial Revolution in American Business* (Cambridge: Belknap Press, 1977).
[2] Adolf A. Berle, Jr. and Gardiner C. Means, *The Modern Corporation and Private Property* (New York: Macmillan, 1933).

The nature of separation and its degree got an extra push from American populist politics, which kept American financial institutions—banks and insurers at the turn of the twentieth century—small, weak, and generally without authority to own stock. Had the banks and insurers been large and capable of owning stock, they could have played a larger role inside the large firm, as they did in other nations and as institutional investors—as their successors—are playing now in the early twenty-first century.[3]

B. The Advantages

The advantages of separation are clear and need little repeating. Separation allows for a scale of operation far beyond any individual's capacity to provide capital. Even Bill Gates, the richest American, owns only 10 percent of Microsoft. Distant outsiders, and a few other insiders, own the rest. Moreover, separation allows firms to combine managers with talent but without much capital (at least initially) with investors who have capital but neither the time nor the skills to manage. It provides founders a key exit strategy; exit barriers are also entry barriers, and if founders did not have a range of exits, entrepreneurial activity would presumably be weaker than it is in the United States. Separation also allows investors to diversify, facilitating more efficient savings over time. And it facilitates product market competition, by easing the financing needs of start-ups and new entrants.

▶ *The advantages of separation [of ownership and control of the corporation] are clear. It allows for a scale of operation far beyond any individual's capacity to provide capital. It provides founders a key exit strategy. It allows owners to diversify, facilitating more efficient savings over time. And it facilitates product market competition, by easing the financing needs of start-ups and new entrants.*

---

[3] Mark J. Roe, *Strong Managers, Weak Owners: The Political Roots of American Corporate Governance* (Princeton: Princeton University Press, 1994). And then we would have faced a different sort of separation, one that would have focused more on financial institutions—and hence on the separation between savers and the institution's portfolio—and less on corporate ownership.

C. The Recurring Breakdowns

But separation's advantages come with costs. The most significant cost that repeatedly destabilizes corporate governance is
that with ownership separated from management, managers'
control of the firm can lead to poor results. No one might check
them. Managers' goals sometimes deteriorate into just wanting
to be paid well, to live well, and to keep those operations going
that they understand, instead of doing the hard work of innovat-
ing for the firm, its stockholders, and American consumers.
Without anyone checking, the problems might fester. More
importantly, technologies and markets change, and sometimes
the incumbent managers aren't the right ones to handle the
change. But with ownership separated from control, they hang
on for longer than is good for the economy.

Concentrated shareholding reduces separation's problems
but comes with its own costs, mostly by enhancing the risk that
insiders shift value from outside shareholders to themselves.
Other nations face this problem more than we do. There's no
"silver bullet."

We can see a series of American corporate crises in the half-
century or so since World War II, all emanating from the core
difficulty of separation. Our Enron and WorldCom crises are
just the latest manifestation of the underlying fissure, the
inevitable cost that comes with the benefits of separation. In the
1950s, the crisis was in the corporation's—and its managers'—
overwhelming power in society, power that came when separation combined with domestic oligopoly that didn't yet face
strong international competitors. In the 1960s, it was the large
corporations' impulse to expand sales without regard to profits,
innovation, or consumer well-being, often resulting in unwieldy
conglomerates. Hostile takeovers burst on the scene in the late
1970s, and had become by the 1980s a *cause célèbre* of corporate,
political, and social debate. In their best manifestation, they
were the means to reduce the costs of separation, and make
managers more responsive to markets. In their worst interpretation, they were the means by which greedy managers expanded
their corporate empires. And by the end of the 1980s the insider

trading scandals—centering on Ivan Boesky, Michael Milken, and a few others—were seen in the press, and perhaps by the public, as central to a tawdry corporate system. In the late 1990s, executive compensation—exemplified by CEO Michael Eisner's infamously large 1999 paycheck from Disney—seemed out of control. And then in the twenty-first century's first decade we've had Enron, WorldCom, and associated failures, in which managers misstated their numbers, and their accountant watchdogs' eyes were closed. Or worse.

Each decade had its crisis, and each crisis had its quintessential academic analysts. And each crisis, and the analytic movement it precipitated, can be traced back to the separation of ownership from control, occasionally via a reaction, or overreaction, to the prior crisis. Let's review each breakdown in more detail.

1. Managerial power in the 1950s. The issue in the 1950s was power. Consider a primary academic document of that time, Edward Mason's edited collection of essays, *The Corporation in Modern Society.*[4] (Mason was an economics professor at Harvard who had brought together a group of corporate thinkers to contemplate the 1950s firm.) The consensus view then was that the large corporation was a powerful creature that had to be tamed. Otherwise it would trample its employees, its customers, and its communities. It was too powerful, and the polity had to watch it warily. Public policy should be, it was thought, directed to taming and caging the firm.

Mason himself said: "This powerful corporate machine, which so successfully grinds out the goods we want, seems to be running without any discernible controls."[5] Others said that the corporation had "produced a tension of power ... [as] giant enterprises ... come to rival the sovereignty of the state itself."[6] Looking back, I'd

[4] Edward Mason, ed., *The Corporation in Modern Society* (Cambridge: Harvard University Press, 1959). More detail on this era can be found in Mark J. Roe, "From Antitrust to Corporate Governance? The Corporation and the Law: 1959–1994," in Carl Kaysen, ed., *The American Corporation Today* (Oxford: Oxford University Press, 1996), 102–127.

[5] Mason, ed., *The Corporation in Modern Society*, 3–4.

[6] Earl Latham, "The Body Politic of the Corporation," in Mason, ed., *The Corporation in Modern Society*, 218.

say that oligopolistic slack in the product markets had combined with ownership separation to give managers at the large firms—GM, GE, IBM—enormous power and discretion.

That power arose from the large American firms' command over capital, from their size, and from their insulation from strong competition in American oligopolistic markets that lacked serious international competition. Separation gave them discretion, and separation gave them freedom to build over-sized firms. The Big Three automakers, Big Steel, and the electrical equipment manufacturers were powerful firms with powerful managers who enjoyed discretion over what to do with above-normal profits. Managerial discretion—from separation—and big profits made the power of American managers salient in the 1950s. Would the powerful captains of industry distribute those supra-normal profits to themselves—via high salaries, nice offices, and a quiet life? Or to shareholders, to employees, to charity, or to customers via a better product?

> ▶ *The sense of overweening managerial power [in the 1950s] faded. Antitrust policy was the central remedy in academic analyses [then]. Perhaps merger policy—the Justice Department and court decisions barred most big horizontal and vertical mergers during the era—made a difference, and academic analysts of the time hoped it would. But the rise of international competitors also affected American managerial power, perhaps more so.*

That sense of overweening power faded. Antitrust policy was the central remedy in academic analyses in the 1950s and early 1960s. Perhaps merger policy—the Justice Department and court decisions barred most big horizontal and vertical mergers during the era—made a difference, and academic analysts of the time hoped it would. But the rise of international competitors in manufacturing also affected American managerial power, perhaps more so. Heightened competition and rapidly changing technologies changed managers from the all-powerful players the academics found them to be in the 1950s, to misdirected builders of unwieldy conglomerates by the 1970s, and then to failures at reconstructing their firms in the 1980s.

But at the core of the perceived problem of the 1950s was ownership separation. Separation and strong profits gave those firms' managers discretion over an enormous pool of profits and capital that far exceeded the individual wealth of any of them. They could build and run big, over-sized firms. They seemed powerful, and they were.

2. *Expanding, satisficing, and maximizing sales in the 1960s and 1970s.* By the late 1960s and early 1970s, the perception changed from power to waste. Firms spent too much on advertising, provided too many quickly-obsolete products, and expanded for size, not profits. Managerialism was still front and center, but the dominant sense then—reflected in Oliver Williamson's classics—was that managers maximized their power, prestige, and salaries by maximizing sales. As to profits, they merely *satisficed*. Managers couldn't ignore profits entirely, but as long as they were in an acceptable range, it was sales that they sought to maximize.[7]

3. *The conglomerates in the 1960s and 1970s.* Bloat and discretion had their quintessential corporate form: the American conglomerate of that era. A headquarters of strategic thinkers would direct the far-flung subsidiaries in the multi-divisional corporation. Local managers would have local information and skills, while the central managers had vision and the capacity to allocate capital. For a time the conglomerate was not seen as a problem, but as a solution to ownership separation, as the central managers at headquarters would monitor the operating managers in the divisions and subsidiaries, giving the stars more capital and squeezing money out of the weaker divisions. This state of affairs—and the conglomerates' capacity to reduce separation's managerial problems—was briefly celebrated in economics circles.[8]

[7] Oliver E. Williamson, *The Economics of Discretionary Behavior: Managerial Objectives in a Theory of the Firm* (Englewood Cliffs, N.J.: Prentice Hall, 1964). See also Robin Marris, *The Economic Theory of "Managerial" Capitalism* (London: Macmillan, 1964); Herbert A. Simon, "Theories of Bounded Rationality," in C. B. McGuire and Roy Radner, eds., *Decision and Organization* (Amsterdam: North Holland, 1972); Richard M. Cyert and James G. March, *A Behavioral Theory of the Firm* (Princeton: Prentice Hall, 1962).

[8] Oliver E. Williamson, *Markets and Hierarchies: Analysis and Antitrust Implications: A Study in the Economics of Internal Organization* (New York: Free Press, 1975).

4. Hostile takeovers and competitive failure in the 1970s and 1980s.
By the 1980s, the large American manufacturing firm looked like
it was on the ropes. Powerful European and Japanese competitors were out-producing their American rivals. Oligopolistic
profits were gone, as the big firms in industry after industry had
to compete with tough players from overseas. Something had to
be done to squeeze out corporate bloat, to make the American
firm lean, mean, and competitive once again, to dismantle the
slow-moving conglomerates. Conglomerates were no longer the
solution to the separation fissure, they were its biggest problem.

The market and theory also gave us a mechanism to reduce
separation's then-current critical problem—the conglomerate
and the misdirected manager—via the hostile takeover. The
takeover entrepreneur would buy up the firm's stock, sell off the
divisions separately, and then make a profit because the pieces
could be better managed separately than jointly in the slack-
heavy conglomerate; so buyers would pay more for the better-
managed separate divisions, enough to cover the costs of the
takeover. This possibility was celebrated in financial analyses,
most prominently by Michael Jensen.[9] Leveraged buyouts
would focus managers' attention on a single firm with a single
product, reducing separation's problems.

Counter-arguments arose. Firms needed to make commitments to their employees, and a deep hostile takeover market
made managerial commitments worthless, because the managers
could be thrown out. In the public arena, a key issue was seen to
be that takeovers broke implicit promises that managers made to
employees, who thought they had an understanding that they
would keep their jobs as long as they did their work well, not
just for as long as markets—financial, product, and takeover—
agreed. And some takeovers were done not to dismantle the
bloated conglomerate, but to build more power for the offering
managers. But wherever one stood on these issues, the source of
the problem was clear: it was again the separation of ownership
from control.

[9] Michael C. Jensen, "Agency Costs of Free Cash Flow, Corporate Finance, and
Takeovers," *American Economic Review Papers & Proceedings* 76 (1986): 323.

5. Insider trading in the 1980s. Separation meant those trading stock would often have less information than those inside the corporation. Often that disparity of information wasn't very important, because the insiders didn't know much that would change the value of the stock. Though cases of unlawful insider trading arose intermittently and others presumably went undetected, the problem seemed decidedly second-order.

The explosion of takeovers changed that. Players who got wind of a takeover at a big premium had information that they could trade on profitably. They could buy stock from naïve, distant individual investors at low prices, and then make a bundle when the offer was announced. Not only did inside managers have this information, but so did inside Wall Street professionals—and the Wall Streeters knew how to trade fast and well. The burst of inside trading led to headlines, indictments—most famously of Michael Milken, the junk bond trader, and Ivan Boesky, the arbitrageur—and demeaned the legitimacy of the stock market in the eyes of many.[10]

6. Executive pay in the 1990s. In 1999, Michael Eisner's pay was more than $500 million, including profits from the stock options he cashed in.[11] Some thought that excessive, and his paycheck got headlines and media attention; others thought it a just reward for the shareholder value he initially created.[12] Executive pay rose then both in absolute and relative terms. Executive pay was about 40 times the average worker's pay from the 1950s to 1980.[13] After a sustained rise in executive pay during the 1990s, CEO compensation rose from 140 times to *500 times* the average

---

[10] Milken was not indicted for insider trading, but for securities violations arising from "parking" stock.

[11] See "Forbes Executive Pay," available at www.forbes.com/lists.

[12] See Elizabeth Smith, "This is Not Michael Eisner's Pay Stub...," *Fortune* (June 8, 1998): 294; "Who Wants to Be a Billionaire?," *The Economist* (May 8, 1999); "Who Earned the Pay—And Who Didn't," *Business Week* (April 19, 1999): 75. Some commentators thought that Disney's stock performance justified the pay; indeed, by tying compensation to performance, the high compensation may have caused the excellent financial results. The paycheck was still controversial.

[13] "Face Value: Business as the New Rock and Roll," *The Economist* (November 28, 1998): 70; John A. Byrne, "What, Me Overpaid? CEOs Fight Back," *Business Week* (May 4, 1992): 142–143.

employee's pay by 2003.[14] Explanations are several. The pay could have been efficient, in better aligning senior managers with stockholders.[15] The pay rewarded modern executives for the excess risks that managers faced in a volatile 1990s, when executive turnover was rapid. The CEO got paid well, but, like a star athlete, would only keep that job for a few years.[16]

Or the pay resulted from ownership separation. No one was checking managers closely; norms had changed; and executives could now cash in on their power inside the firm.[17]

7. And Enron in the twenty-first century. And then came Enron. Enron's managers, most notably Chief Financial Officer Andrew Fastow, misstated their firm's numbers, in ways that moved funds out from Enron and into their own pockets, and no one caught it. Enron's obligations via the related special purpose vehicle financings weren't stated in Enron's financials. The board's audit committee didn't catch the problem; the board suspended the firm's own conflict-of-interest rules; and the firm's accountants didn't react to the problem. Separation meant that those watching internally—the board and its committees— weren't watching their own money. With specialization they depended on others for information—primarily lower-ranking managers inside the firm, like Fastow, but also outsiders—and those others didn't provide it well. While Enron's fraud in using the related entities—the special purpose vehicles—was novel in its specifics, WorldCom's financial misstatements were more ordinary—just big.

---

[14] Janice Ravel, "Mo' Money, Fewer Problems: Is it a Good Idea to Get Rid of the $1 Million CEO Pay Ceiling?" *Fortune* (March 31, 2003): 34.
[15] Brian J. Hall and Jeffrey B. Liebman, "Are CEOs Really Paid like Bureaucrats?" *Quarterly Journal of Economics* 63 (1998): 653; Kevin Murphy, "Executive Compensation," in Orley Ashenfelter and David Card, eds., *Handbook of Labor Economics* (Amsterdam: North Holland, 1999).
[16] Rakesh Khurana, *Searching for a Corporate Savior: The Irrational Quest for Charismatic CEOs* (Princeton: Princeton University Press, 2002).
[17] Lucian A. Bebchuk and Jesse M. Fried, "Executive Compensation as an Agency Problem," *Journal of Economics Perspectives* 17 (2003): 71–92; Lucian A. Bebchuk and Jesse M. Fried, *Pay Without Performance: The Unfulfilled Promise of Executive Compensation* (Cambridge: Harvard University Press, 2004); Michael C. Jensen and Kevin J. Murphy, "CEO Incentives—It's Not How Much You Pay, But How," *Harvard Business Review* 68 (May-June 1990): 138–149.

So when ownership separates from control, problems arise. Managers pursue their own agenda, and it seems that in every decade there's been a systematic failure. Combine separation with oligopoly and we got enormous power in the 1950s. Combine separation with ideas about conglomerates and we got mega-firms without continued justification in the 1960s. We got solutions—like hostile takeovers—against which the public reacted in the 1980s. We got hyper-pay in the 1990s, which was partly a solution and partly a resultant problem. And in the beginning of the 21st century we got misstated financial statements that undermined confidence in stock markets, and made the mis-staters (temporarily) rich.

We haven't been able to fully stabilize the collateral damage from ownership separation. Weaknesses appeared, became toxic, and then we had to cure and repair. But we would do better than we have thus far—or at least we would have a differing set of primary problems—were it not for the negative effects of the second major instability in American corporate governance: the porous nature of regulation. American regulation is open and decentralized, and those qualities give the regulated—often the very managers whom we are trying to direct toward efficiency and away from scurrilous behavior—the capacity to influence, and often weaken, that regulation.

II. THE POROSITY OF AMERICAN REGULATION

A. The Decentralized Structure

1. Federalism. The United States doesn't have a centralized "czar" whose job it is to regulate corporate governance. Often this decentralization is celebrated, especially when it's in the form of state competition for corporate charters, and the concomitant regulation of the corporation via state corporate law.[18] That

---

[18] Roberta Romano, *The Genius of American Corporate Law* (Washington, D.C.: AEI Press, 1993). Not everyone is happy with this decentralization, with many analysts thinking it leads to rules that overly favor managers. William L. Cary, "Federalism and Corporate Law: Reflections upon Delaware," *Yale Law Journal* 83 (1974): 663,

state-based regulation tends to come through contractual enabling—the corporate charter can be built in almost any way that the participants prefer—and judge-enforced fiduciary duties. Regulatory commissions and criminal actions are largely absent in making state corporate law.[19]

That said, corporate governance is also federal, via the securities laws and the SEC. True, the SEC's power here is incomplete, mostly centered on disclosure and trading in the securities markets. But corporate governance can be deeply affected by simple disclosure. That is, most states have some rule or another against thievery and interested party transactions. The transactional problem is how to get that information out from inside the corporation. Mandatory disclosure rules, mandatory accounting rules, and SEC control (or influence) over the accounting profession can—when the SEC acts properly and is adequately funded—deeply affect corporate governance.[20]

> ▶ *The United States doesn't have a centralized "czar" whose job it is to regulate corporate governance. This fragmented nature sometimes allows one regulator to check the other. It also avoids [much] over-regulation.*

2. *Further fragmentation.* And then there's Congress. It acts sporadically in corporate governance, but it does act. And courts sometimes interpret key provisions of the securities or other federal laws to make corporate policy. Moreover, some elements of corporate governance are self-regulatory: The New York Stock

705; Lucian Arye Bebchuk, "Federalism and the Corporation: The Desirable Limits on State Competition in Corporate Law," *Harvard Law Review* 105 (1992): 1437, 1509.
[19] Cf. Mark J. Roe, "Delaware's Advantage" (working paper, 2004).
[20] Mark J. Roe, "Delaware's Competition," *Harvard Law Review* 117 (2003): 588–646. Cf. William W. Bratton, "Corporate Law's Race to Nowhere in Particular," *University of Toronto Law Journal* 44 (1994): 401, 419; John C. Coffee, Jr., "The Future of Corporate Federalism: State Competition and the New Trend Toward De Facto Federal Minimum Standards," *Cardozo Law Review* 8 (1987): 759, 768; Melvin Eisenberg, "The Structure of Corporation Law," *Columbia Law Review* 89 (1989): 1461, 1512; Arthur Fleischer, Jr., "Federal Corporation Law: An Assessment," *Harvard Law Review* 78 (1965): 1146 (federal disclosure rules control fiduciary behavior); Mark J. Roe, "Takeover Politics," in Margaret Blair, ed., *The Deal Decade* (Washington, D.C.: Brookings Institution Press, 1993), 321, 340–347.

Exchange makes governance rules, though often after SEC prodding. And private codes of conduct arise from time to time.

This fragmented nature sometimes allows one regulator to check the other; if one state doesn't act, then maybe the New York Attorney General will swing into action. If states are in managers' palms, then maybe an SEC with overall American economic performance in mind will use its bully pulpit to induce action, or might act directly itself.

But the fragmented nature of regulation also allows some potential innovation and cross-checking to fall unused through the cracks. Stock exchange officials might consider forensic audits to be a good idea, but the stock exchanges could think it's someone else's job to push for it. Delaware's judges bemoan the fact that they can't do the fact-finding and prospective regulation that a regulatory agency could undertake.[21] That is, one of our most important corporate governance regulators can only act after the fact, when private parties bring it a case to decide. The SEC could bemoan its lack of full power over the public corporation; it might have lots of good ideas, but the securities laws give it only incomplete authority, and the Business Roundtable (and the business lobby more generally) stands ready to remind the SEC (and, if necessary, the federal courts) of the limits to the SEC's power.

B. The Inevitably Porous Structure

1. The conceptual issues. Fragmentation obviously has its advantages and its disadvantages. One can't say in the abstract which is better, fragmentation or centralization. On the plus side, we don't suffer from an unchecked, monolithic regulator. And we usually don't suffer from too much over-regulation. Differing regulators have differing sources of information, differing regulatory styles, and differing modes of enforcement. The regulated can interact with the regulators to bring to bear the information they have to make the resulting regulation better than it would otherwise be and to avoid a regulator's tendency to over-regu-

---

[21] One wonders why they don't ask the Delaware legislature to set up a corporate law regulatory agency.

late. It's easy for a regulator to be too tough on boards of directors. The regulator gets credit for solving the problem, but then the boards become less attractive for directors to join, or less effective in running the nation's business. Pushback from the regulated reduces over-regulation.

But decentralization, even if good on balance, is not good in all respects. Some items may fall through the cracks, and that might be the price we pay for the advantages of decentralization. But the regulated have a deep impact on the fragmented regulators and that raises the costs even higher.

(a) In Delaware. Everyone agrees that managers strongly influence the making of Delaware's corporate law. While the judiciary is independent, the legislature can, and sometimes does, overturn the courts. And the Delaware legislature acts after a bar association committee—drawn from leaders of the law firms that represent managers and sometimes investors—recommends action. The agreement on managerial influence is wide; the difference in opinion is on whether that influence is pernicious or, overall, beneficial.[22] Perhaps managerial influence explains why, for better or worse, Delaware is not seen as a tough regulator, why it doesn't use criminal penalties for corporate governance misdeeds, and why it has no forward-looking powerful regulator.

More generally, consider how the states, and Delaware in particular, responded to takeovers in the 1980s. Conceptually takeovers can be seen as a key way to reduce the costs of ownership separation; mediocre managers would find their stock price dropping. Outsiders would buy up the stock, fire the managers, reconstruct the firm to be profitable, and thereby make the takeover pay for them. But target firm managers disliked takeovers. So they lobbied state legislatures to bar them, often successfully. Takeovers were one way to reduce the costs of sepa-

[22] And, actually, some are less certain of how independent the judiciary always is. Judges are picked after vetting by bar associations and law firms, after their corporate loyalty is tested. See William L. Cary, "Federalism and Corporate Law: Reflections upon Delaware," *Yale Law Journal* 83 (1974): 663; Jonathan R. Macey and Geoffrey P. Miller, "Toward an Interest-Group Theory of Delaware Corporate Law," *Texas Law Review* 65 (1987): 469, 473.

ration, but the regulated affected how easily takeovers could occur. Most states passed laws that made hostile takeovers much harder, and managers' lobbying was central to getting those laws enacted.[23] And while Delaware was slow to enact an anti-takeover law, it did come around, and managerial influence was quite visible.

(b) In Congress. Congress can regulate corporate governance. But its members run for election, and they need campaign contributions.

Takeovers again provide an example. In the 1980s, hostile takeovers were central to American corporate governance. In the late 1980s, Congress considered legislation that would have barred many of managers' defensive measures. Lobbying by the Business Roundtable—big firms' lobbying organization—probably affected the outcomes of what passed, or more accurately, didn't pass.

▶ *Congress can regulate corporate governance. But its members run for election, and they need campaign contributions. Moreover, Congress can control other regulators, like the SEC. Managers who face a loss with the SEC can lobby Congress to rein the SEC in.*

Moreover, Congress can control other regulators, like the SEC. Managers who face a loss with the SEC can lobby Congress to rein the SEC in.

(c) Via information and lobbying. The regulated can bring forward and highlight the negative aspects of any proposed regulation of themselves, or any looming empowerment of their gatekeeper-watchers. In the balance, the proposed regulation could then seem less wise than it otherwise would look.

In 1991, the SEC proposed loosening up the then-severe restrictions on institutional investor action, some of which continue today. At that time, if institutional investors talked widely

---

[23] Roe, *Strong Managers*, 151–168; Roe, "Takeover Politics," in Blair, ed., *The Deal Decade*, 340–347; Joseph A. Grundfest, "Subordination of American Capital," *Journal of Financial Economics* 27 (1990): 89–114; Roberta Romano, "The Political Economy of Takeover Statutes," *Virginia Law Review* 73 (1987): 11. Some state legislators surely thought takeovers were bad policy. And others responded to target firm employees' interests, not just managerial interests. But no one would deny that managers were important lobbyists for state anti-takeover laws.

enough about dysfunctional boards and how some board members should be turned out, they risked criminal prosecution for failing to file a proxy statement. (While the risk of real criminal prosecution was low, the real risk of some SEC enforcement action and its concomitant embarrassment was enough to deter activity.) The securities laws required a proxy filing when shareholders communicated with the intention, or as part of a plan, to change control of a corporation. When the SEC first brought forward its plan to loosen up the rigid rules here, managers spoke of smoke-filled back-room deals among institutional investors to the detriment of small stockholders.[24] The SEC withdrew its proposed rule and, for a time, it seemed dead. Then the SEC came back with a weaker but still viable version, and promulgated that rule.[25]

Another instance is the American Law Institute's effort to promulgate standards for corporate governance that would tighten up the structure of the American corporation at its top. The Institute is run neither solely by ivory tower professors nor by regulators fully separated from the regulated. Business lawyers—managers' representatives, corporate counsel, and so on—are big players, and they defeated several proposals to tighten up corporate governance. Reformers trying to draft the ALI Corporate Governance rules "were opposed by a cohesive group of corporate counsel and the companies who employed them. The ALI ultimately adopted a vague rule that permitted directors and state courts to do what they had previously been doing."[26] We have a looser system—for good or ill—partly

[24] "Business Roundtable Criticizes SEC Plan on Shareholder Data," *Wall Street Journal*, September 20, 1991, A4.
[25] Stephen Labaton, "U.S. Pressed by Business Over S.E.C," *New York Times*, October 18, 1991, D1: The Business Roundtable met with the administration to bypass the SEC "in trying to prevent new rules for corporate shareholder battles." The Roundtable also attacked the SEC's proposed rules as allowing back-room corporate deals. See also Roberta S. Karmel, "CalPERS versus the Business Roundtable," *New York Law Journal* (February 21, 1991): 3.
[26] Alan Schwartz and Robert E. Scott, "The Political Economy of Private Legislatures," *University of Pennsylvania Law Review* 143 (1995): 595–642. Similarly, Stephen M. Bainbridge, "Independent Directors and the ALI Corporate Governance Project," *George Washington Law Review* 61 (1993): 1034, 1044, 1048, 1052. Bainbridge reports that it was alleged "that corporations were hiring members of the ALI to rep-

because it's the managers' representatives who drafted, or had to approve, many of the rules and quasi-rules.

(d) Via litigation. The regulated can attack regulation that would better align managers and insiders with stockholders. One well-known example is the SEC's effort to reduce insider power by barring recapitalizations that led to insiders having more votes per share of stock than outsiders. Such recapitalizations were at the time a common method for target firm stockholders to resist hostile takeover offers; they kept enough votes for themselves to stop takeovers that other shareholders might have wanted. The Business Roundtable opposed the rule. When the SEC promulgated it anyway, the Roundtable attacked the SEC's rule as exceeding the SEC's authority under the securities laws. They won.[27]

2. The recent examples. Both the run-up to the Enron scandals and the regulatory reaction display America's porosity in regulating corporate governance. Some of it is on the positive side: Congress reacted proactively via the Sarbanes-Oxley Act of 2002, and Delaware has gotten tougher on insiders since the scandals broke. The New York Attorney General swung into action, and the SEC has begun to consider rules that would further regulate managers and accountants. Multiple regulators offered multiple solutions, emanating from their specialized strengths.

But not all porosity was good. Accountants as lobbyists with Congress had held off the SEC from reducing accountants' conflicts of interests. The regulated in general—managers as well as accountants—watched as an anti-regulatory Congress starved the SEC of funding.[28] Managers at first slowed Sarbanes-Oxley

resent their interests in that body's deliberations and that they were removing their legal business from law firms with partners who were sympathetic to the ALI's pro-litigation outlook." See also Jonathan R. Macey, "The Transformation of the American Law Institute," *George Washington Law Review* 61 (1993): 1212, 1228–1232.

[27] *Business Roundtable v. SEC*, 905 F.2d 406, 407 (D.C. Cir. 1990). The Roundtable at least won the battle. The SEC eventually induced the stock exchanges to promulgate one-share, one-vote rules.

[28] David E. Rovella, "Congressional Ploys Squeeze SEC Budget; A fight over the agency's budget creates fiscal crisis," *National Law Journal*, September 5, 1994. Congress cut the SEC's funding request from $305 million to $125 million. And

reforms in Congress. One reformer—John Biggs—was blocked from taking over the regulation of the accounting gatekeepers. And managers and their regulatory allies have thus far stopped the SEC from tightening up corporate governance in a way that would heighten shareholder oversight.

Let's look at these in more detail.

(a) Accountants and Congress. Accountants were auditing their clients and selling them consulting services, often of tax strategy or in information systems. Managers could influence their gate-keepers by turning the consulting revenue spigots open, or by closing them.[29] Arthur Levitt, the chair of the SEC, wanted to break this conflict. In June 2000, the SEC proposed rules to separate auditing from consulting.

But the accountants lobbied Congress to stop Levitt. They succeeded.[30] Levitt's abortive effort here is instructive. Congress, in effect, told Levitt not to go forward, threatening both to cut SEC funding further and to reduce SEC authority. The SEC cannot resist a determined Congress. And this time at least, the gatekeepers got to Congress. Levitt watered down the new rules, and didn't separate auditing from consulting.[31]

(b) Silicon Valley's stock options. Silicon Valley liked to pay employees in stock options. If the firm's stock soared, the employees got rich. But the firms didn't like to deduct the value of the stock option as a cost of operating their firm. The accountants' regulatory organization, the Financial Accounting Standards Board (usually known as FASB) decided that employee pay in cash and employee pay in stock options were each still pay that was an expense to the corporation. Expenses had to be deducted from income. They moved toward requiring the value

Congress also nixed the SEC's plea to fund itself with further user fees: "Sen. Phil Gramm, R-Texas, who led the Republican effort to scuttle self-funding, said SEC independence 'would only increase the likelihood of escalating fees on the securities markets' and make the agency less responsive to Congress."

[29] Jeffrey N. Gordon, "What Enron Means for the Management and Control of the Modern Business Corporation: Some Initial Reflections," *University of Chicago Law Review* 69 (1992): 1233–1250.

[30] For a critical reportorial account, see Mike Brewster, *Unaccountable: How the Accounting Profession Forfeited a Public Trust* (New York: John Wiley & Sons, 2003).

[31] Brewster, *Unaccountable: How the Accounting Profession Forfeited a Public Trust.*

of employee stock options to be deducted from a firm's accounting profits.

But FASB never required American firms to deduct the value
of options given to employees. Why? The regulated—here,
Silicon Valley, the prime users of stock options—got to the regulators, this time through Congress:

> Following an intense lobbying campaign by Silicon
> Valley companies, several leading members of Congress,
> including Joseph Lieberman and Diane Feinstein,
> threatened to put the F.A.S.B. out of business if it went
> ahead with the change. The board backed down, [and
> thus that] ... official attempt to control corporate
> avarice came to an end.[32]

As Donald Langevoort points out in this volume, this ability
of the regulated to influence the regulators further rationalized
some managerial financial
misreporting.[33] Since the
government backed down,
why should executives try
harder to report financial
results precisely?

▶ *FASB never required American firms to
deduct the value of options given to employees.
Why? The regulated—here, Silicon Valley,
the prime users of stock options—got to the
regulators, this time through Congress.*

And despite the post-
scandal backlash, it's not yet over: The Silicon Valley lobbyists
are still at it, in 2004:

> Silicon Valley was [in July 2004] sitting on ... members
> of Congress, whispering sweet nothings in their ears.
> As in, stock options cost nothing. And 312 members of
> the House listened.
>
> That was the number of congressmen who voted for
> the Baker Bill, a measure that damages efforts of the
> Financial Accounting Standards Board to enact rules

---

[32] John Cassidy, "The Greed Cycle: How the financial system encouraged corporations to go crazy," *The New Yorker*, September 23, 2002, 64, 69. And FASB is a self-
regulatory operation, not an independent imposing regulator. William W. Bratton,
"Rules, Principles, and the Accounting Crisis in the United States," *European Business
Organization Law Review* 5 (2004): 7–25.
[33] At p. 63.

mandating the expensing of stock options. The bill violates FASB's independence….

Not able to fight stock-option expensing completely, Silicon Valley was content with a compromise. Knowing that something is wrong with not expensing any stock options, the writers of the Baker Bill want stock options for only the CEO and the next four highest-paid executives to be expensed.[34]

(c) Cutting funding for the SEC; slowing reform after Enron. In the 1990s, Congress sharply cut funding for the SEC. Much of Congress's early 1990s funding cutbacks arose out of the anti-regulatory thinking then dominating Congress. One aspect is telling: Some in Congress wanted to give the SEC authority to levy higher user fees, which the SEC could then use for its own operating budget. But, said Senator Phil Gramm and his allies, if the SEC could self-finance via user fees it would become more independent from Congress.[35] Gramm won. So the chain persisted: interest groups—like our gatekeepers—can influence Congress, and Congress can control the SEC.

After Enron broke, there was a flurry of reform thinking, but it faded quickly from the congressional agenda, apparently with managerial blessing and lobbying,[36] and didn't seem likely to produce action until WorldCom collapsed. With WorldCom's collapse, members of Congress who had opposed strong regulatory reform changed their minds.

(d) Today: Lobbying the SEC on shareholder access. In the wake of Enron, the SEC concluded that America's boards—the primary gatekeeper of internal managers—would be stronger if stockholders of poorly performing companies could get access to the company's proxy statement to elect a couple of directors.

---

[34] Jess Eisinger, "Microsoft Can Count. Intel Can't," *Wall Street Journal*, July 21, 2004.
[35] "S.E.C. Budget Request Cut," *New York Times*, June 28, 1994; Rovella, "Congressional Ploys Squeeze SEC Budget; A fight over the agency's budget creates fiscal crisis."
[36] William Neikirk, "Andersen: The Fallout," *Chicago Tribune*, June 18, 2002 (corporate lobbying to stall reform).

Nothing dramatic, but a tilt toward opening up the boardroom. (The usual American practice is that incumbent managers get their nomination and reelection expenses paid for by the company itself; others nominating directors have to pay their own expenses, which typically amount to millions of dollars.) British shareholders may remove directors, nearly at will. The SEC proposal would stop far short of that.

But thus far managers have stymied the SEC, pressuring it to back off "in the face of opposition from the Chamber of Commerce and the Business Roundtable, an organization of chief executives from the nation's largest companies."[37] The SEC's retreat was seen as a "major victory for corporate executives who have fought to kill the rule."[38] Managers had beaten back shareholder access proposals over the decades,[39] and thus far seem to have done so again, pushing the SEC back to a weakened version of its original plan.[40] The regulated beat back reform that would have narrowed that gap in the separation of ownership from control, our fundamental fissure. They used information (arguing that the rule wouldn't work well, would disrupt boardrooms, and would be used primarily by special interests) and worst-case scenarios (paralyzed boards or boards dominated by special interests without a shareholder agenda or, worse, with an anti-shareholder agenda[41]), and tapped the Congress and the White House as levers.[42]

[37] Stephen Labaton, "S.E.C. at Odds on Plan to Let Big Investors Pick Directors," *New York Times,* July 1, 2004. See also Adrian Michaels, "Vote on Reforming Boardroom Elections Delayed by SEC Split," *Financial Times,* June 1, 2004; Deborah Solomon, "SEC May Temper Plan to Boost Shareholders' Powers," *Wall Street Journal,* April 19, 2004.
[38] Labaton, "S.E.C. at Odds on Plan to Let Big Investors Pick Directors."
[39] Mortimer M. Caplin, "Proxies, Annual Meetings and Corporate Democracy: The Lawyers' Role," *Virginia Law Review* 37 (1951): 653, 682–684.
[40] Deborah Solomon, "SEC Nears Compromise on Shareholder Plan," *Wall Street Journal,* August 11, 2004.
[41] Presumably they are referring to funds described in Damon Silvers' essay in this volume, at p. 85. When the SEC in 1992 cut back rules that had made it a potentially criminal offense for investors to talk with one another about a bad board, some managerial groups were similarly unhappy with the potential of more gatekeeper oversight. "Big-business leaders blasted the proxy change, contending that it will allow well-heeled shareholders to plot against the interests of companies and smaller holders without notification. It is 'hard to fathom why the commission would allow big,

CONCLUSION

American corporate governance has two inevitable instabilities. With control separated from ownership, managers' agenda differs from that of others inside the corporation; and, especially with ownership fragmented, a few managers sometimes go bad, demeaning their corporations and, if the misconduct is widespread enough, even the economy. Technology changes, crises arise, and the problems in one decade differ from those of another decade. But the principal problems arise from ownership separation, and ownership separation is with us to stay.

Other nations have less ownership separation but that comes with another set of problems, mostly those that arise from concentrated ownership (via insider machinations) and weak stock markets (because one key financing source is less viable). To say that our problems derive from separation isn't to say that we can do better by giving up separation. It just says that we have to deal repeatedly with separation's derivative problems.

Thus we fix up each current problem, and we muddle through.[43] We'll further professionalize directors, as called for in the essay in this volume by Martin Lipton and Jay W. Lorsch.[44]

powerful investors the right to line up votes for a proxy contest . . . without some kind of public disclosure to the other shareholders,' said . . . an official of the Business Roundtable[.]" Kevin Salwen, "SEC Votes to Ease Barriers to Holders' Communications," *Wall Street Journal*, October 16, 1992.

[42] Adrian Michaels, "Board Election Rules Debate Defies Unanimity," *Financial Times*, June 16, 2004: "The SEC has entered . . . mainstream politics. The issue of proxy access involves pressure from the White House. The Business Roundtable is crucial to [the Bush administration's] fund-raising." The quotation was of John Coffee, professor of law at Columbia Law School. Cf. Adrian Michaels, "Vote on reforming boardroom elections delayed by SEC split," *Financial Times*, June 1, 2004 (the shareholder access proposals "have pitted powerful business lobbyists against activist institutional investors"). "Opponents of the proposals, such as the Business Roundtable, the powerful chief executive grouping, and the US Chamber of Commerce, say the plans would cause significant disruption even at well-run companies." Michaels, "Vote on reforming boardroom elections delayed by SEC split."

[43] Cf. Charles E. Lindblom, "The Science of 'Muddling Through,'" *Public Administration Review* 19 (1959): 79–88.

[44] At p. 71. See also Margaret Blair's essay at p. 79, and Michael Klausner's paper at p. 91. John S. Reed's essay, at p. 35, also calls for professionalization, although not with that vocabulary. Richard W. Painter, at p. 127, is skeptical as to whether self-regulatory "clubs"—he focuses primarily on lawyers—can be effective without good regulation. Those ideas might extend to wondering whether professionalization of

But comprehensive, once-and-for-all "solutions" to the enduring challenges of American corporate governance are implausible. So we go for ad hoc and partial solutions, like more professionalization and some of the Sarbanes-Oxley regulation, and then we move on.

The essays that follow properly look at the breakdowns in gatekeepers that led to Enron and the associated scandals, and the "Recommendations for Practice" set forth in the Report of the American Academy's Corporate Responsibility Steering Committee[45] suggest how we can improve gatekeeper performance.[46] The gatekeepers are there because managers and boards need to be checked. It's the board and managerial breakdown in the Enron, WorldCom, and the other big scandals that was primary. The gatekeepers were backstops.

▶ *To say that our problems derive from separation isn't to say that we can do better by giving up separation. It just says that we have to deal repeatedly with separation's derivative problems.*

And the first instability interacts with the second one. American corporate governance is porous. We have multiple regulators, each with strengths and weaknesses. Moreover, the regulated often affect how they're regulated. Some of the breakdowns in the gatekeepers, and in the efforts to shore them up, emanated from the actions of the core group to be controlled—often American managers themselves, sometimes accountants, sometimes promoters of Silicon Valley start-ups. The regulated often sought to weaken the regulation that would have reduced their—the managers'—discretion. Shareholders—diffuse and distant—have thus far been less well organized both in affecting firms and in affecting regulators and regulations, although that

directors, alone, without good supporting regulation will work effectively. In their paper at p. 43, Rakesh Khurana and his co-authors advocate the professionalization of corporate management.

[45] At p. 161.

[46] Consider also the essays by William R. Kinney, at p. 99, and John H. Biggs, at p. 109 (both on accountants); William T. Allen and Geoffrey Miller, at p. 113 (on lawyers); Felix G. Rohatyn, at p. 135, and Gerald Rosenfeld, at p. 139 (both on investment bankers); and Geneva Overholser, at p. 145 (on journalists).

may change. Some of this weakness in regulation and the regulators may well be good. It reduces rigidity. It facilitates change and entrepreneurial innovation. It gives us multiple informational channels into the regulators, so that the rules that emerge are more likely to be useful.

But not all porosity is good. Some of it has stopped government players from correcting breakdowns that derive from the separation of ownership from control, because the regulated often seek to deter not just bad regulation, but *any* regulation. Some of the gatekeeper breakdowns that the essays in this volume analyze might have been prevented had gatekeepers and managers not influenced regulators in ways that diminished the gatekeepers' effectiveness. The point here is not that centralization beats decentralization; centralization has its costs, and the regulatory difficulties in other countries display them. The point is that decentralization is our problem, not that there's a fundamental, once-and-for-all solution to the problem.

When Congress acts, in some odd ways it has reason to overreact in the very way that the regulated often fear: when it can act, because the issue is salient, public servants may think that porosity will allow the regulated in the future to beat back some of the rules. So public servants may actually seek more rigidity than is ideal, to reduce future erosion. Put the package together—the regulated as able to affect the regulators and weaken their output, and regulators who when able to act think they must lock it all in—and we've made for more brittleness in corporate governance regulation than would be ideal.

This won't be the last time that corporate governance breaks and cracks in a key way. Different stress points will develop in the public firm, and one or another of the persisting fissures will threaten to open, crack, and need to be fixed. If we're lucky, someone will anticipate the problem and fix it up beforehand. If not, we'll muddle through once again. It's worked so far.

Chapter 2

Values and Corporate Responsibility: A Personal Perspective

JOHN S. REED

All is not well in corporate America. For those of us interested in the practice of management, there are fundamental questions about the overinvestment in telecommunications and media, about the dot-com phenomenon, about financial discipline at firms and at rating agencies, and about the functioning of the financial sector. It seems, indeed, to have been a period of "irrational exuberance." Of greatest concern to all of us is the seemingly broad-based breakdown of values and responsibilities, as highlighted by Enron, WorldCom, Arthur Andersen, the Wall Street "settlement," and so forth. What happened? Why? What is to be done about it?

What happened seems to be clear. At the corporate level, we have seen everything from earnings management to out-and-out fraud, with too many examples of extreme behavior and the complicating complacency of presumed professionals: directors, auditors, lawyers, and bankers. Space does not permit detailed discussion of the cases here; suffice it to say that we have seen "fudged" books, financial gymnastics, off-balance-sheet fictions, questionable income recognition, fictitious "capacity swaps" by telecommunications firms, extraordinary customer financings, and even corporate looting. It is not a pretty picture. Clearly, we have severely harmed the trust and confidence essential to free market capitalism.

In the financial sector, the behavior seems to center on corrupt investment banking. The corruption took the form of bribing potential or actual customers with scarce and profitable initial public offering allocations and, more broadly, buying or providing incentives to analysts to write reports designed to further fuel hot markets and support potential deals. Analysts who were actually part of a retail sales process, presumably acting with brokers and loyal to the buyer, were corrupted into becoming assistants to the investment bankers.

Why this happened is, of course, less clear. Surely incentives were wrong and checks and balances failed to work. My sense is that the seeds of these problems were probably sown back in the 1980s. At the time, corporate America was seen as "stodgy," a "club" uninterested in financial performance, stockholders or product quality, and a "loser" to new international competition—particularly from Japan. This changed. In remarkable ways, investors became the dominant and aggressive feared force. Cynics would say that the balance and judgment expected of management was "bought off" by large stock-based compensation awards with very short-term payoff and limitless bonus payments. The mantra of stockholder value was enshrined in companies, boardrooms, analyst reports, and the business press. Analysts became all-important and stock price became the measure of performance and self-worth (psychologically and literally!). The problem was one of judgment and values. In more cases than we would like to acknowledge, integrity and responsibility were crowded out by shareholder value and the cult of the super-highly paid CEO.

The tensions emanating from the mantra of shareholder value are particularly difficult for the financial community. This community is made up of significantly knowledgeable intermediaries who search for positioning that ranges from (a) that of traditional advisers, willing to say no to a customer if they think a transaction is not in the customer's interest, and unwilling to sell anything in the market that they would not be "willing to put in their mother's account," to (b) that of pure intermediaries, uninterested in anything but matching supply and demand, without reference to their own views on the transaction, and "laying off" any legal or financial risk to themselves through "engineering," to (c) that of aggressive profit seekers operating for their own account, moving beyond the role described in (b) and toward the creation and promotion of transactions on the part of both originators and takers. Society's expectations with regard to these alternatives are not clear; they differ according to the sophistication of the various participants. Also, each of these roles would produce different answers to these questions: Who is the customer? How do loyalties run? In a world of asymmetrical information and competence, these are crucial issues. They are also issues that the industry has not dealt with effectively.

> *The cult of short-term stockholder value has been corrupting. Investors clamoring for performance and share price increases, coupled with unrestrained compensation ("Who cares about bonuses if shareholder value increases?") linked to short-term stock prices, has been demonstrated to be a flawed structure.*

What is to be done? At one level, the problem is a straightforward question of values. Companies are expected to be honest and to report results as they are. Auditors, lawyers, and bankers are expected to maintain values derived from their professions. Investment bankers are also expected to be professionals, and analysts are expected to be, above all, critical thinkers providing the best possible advice to prospective owners of securities. Regulators and boards are expected to be sources of balance and judgment. Individuals are expected to stand up and be independent of "go along" norms.

The cult of short-term stockholder value has been corrupting. Investors clamoring for performance and share price increases, coupled with unrestrained compensation ("Who cares about bonuses if shareholder value increases?") linked to short-term stock prices (by options with short vesting periods), has been demonstrated to be a flawed structure.

Similarly, the link between investment banking and retail distribution, without an overarching management structure that is responsible, visible, and accountable, has proven to be flawed. So too has been the role of boards and the functioning of auditors.

So, at a more profound level, what is to be done? I have a few thoughts:

- Management needs a more wholesome objective than shareholder value. I suggest *evolutionary success*.
- Boards need to accept and be held accountable for new responsibilities, particularly management values and behaviors, and the impact of incentives.
- Structural risks must be offset by clear responsibilities and rules. Those who choose to link investment banking, retail analysis, and distribution must be held to a high standard of performance.
- Auditors and lawyers must be held to be professionals first and foremost. Their expanded activities that raise issues of conflict should be avoided. We can afford to pay the cost of professionalism.
- The final challenge is to surround the enterprise with a self-evaluating and self-correcting process to ensure continuity across time.

MANAGEMENT OBJECTIVE

My own view is that management's objective should not be "shareholder value," which, at least in its current manifestation, is too simplistic, but rather *evolutionary success*. Evolution, a dynamic concept, recognizes the reality of continuous change and adaptation. It incorporates the notion of the environment—customers, competitors, and regulators alike—in defining the determinants of success. It embraces share price (or cost of capital) as a key success factor—but not to the exclusion of other critical success factors, such as bond ratings, research and development expenditures, key trademarks, patents, or human capabilities, each of which has its own role and value.[1]

---

[1] This concept clearly needs greater elaboration than can be fit easily into this paper. Suffice it to say that a thoughtful discussion of evolutionary success would involve identifying key success factors, creating appropriate metrics to capture each, and creating processes to track and evaluate performance and the profile of progress against that set of factors.

A "Report Card" dealing with evolutionary success would be broader and more textured than one limited to shareholder value. It would bring with it more healthy discussion within management, with the board and with the external community. The concept would also embed a more relevant time frame in all these considerations. If well implemented, it would be hard to distort—a problem that turned out to be fatal to shareholder value. (How many boards have said, "Earnings are good, share price is up; all must be well," only to find that they were wrong?)

BOARD RESPONSIBILITY

One of the most striking features of this history is the failure of boards. These bodies and their members are essential as a source of discipline, oversight, balance, and perspective. Shareholders pressure boards to deliver "results"; yet they may fail to appreciate the cost of corrupting the role of these bodies. To solve our problem going forward, I believe that we must rely on individual board members and the board as a group to be *the* guarantors of values, balance, judgment, and accountability.

▶ *My own view is that management's objective should not be "shareholder value," which, at least in its current manifestation, is too simplistic, but rather evolutionary success. Evolution, a dynamic concept, embraces share price (or cost of capital) as a key success factor—but not to the exclusion of other critical success factors.*

We have to look to individual board members, board organization and function, the nature of board discussion, and the board's accountability. My experience is that boards can work, but they do not always work. Board members must be sophisticated and competent, and they cannot be socially or financially beholden to management. That does not mean that a board member cannot have any relationship with the management or the company, or that he or she should be anything but loyal and committed. It just means that relationships should be known, and that they cannot actually be (or be perceived as) debilitating. The distinction is not difficult to make.

Boards must be organized to do their jobs. While it is not vital to distinguish between a chairperson and a CEO, it is vital to recognize that these are two different functions. If a board is to "do its job," the job must be defined. Boards must

- know management's plans and be routinely apprised of progress and problems relating to them;

- understand and be comfortable with the company's strategy and the key underlying assumptions vital to its success, and understand the strategies of the company's competitors;

- understand and be comfortable with the business risks and social expectations for the firm, including control and accounting issues; and

- know the management and be routinely apprised of development and succession plans.

It is clear that in order to do its job, the board must routinely meet in executive session, as well as alone with the CEO; discuss and criticize its own functioning from time to time; and specifically discuss, and be satisfied with, the values and working environment surrounding the senior team, being particularly mindful of the potential problems stemming from compensation and reward practices. Finally, the board should be able to demonstrate to a reasonable degree that it has understood and fulfilled these responsibilities. Errors will be made, but they should not be errors of omission.

Without a clear delineation of the board's responsibilities along these or similar lines, the system is at risk because there will not be any checks and balances.

INVESTMENT BANKING STRUCTURAL RISKS

Origination and distribution, particularly at the retail level, need not be linked in investment banks. Yet they often are, creating the potential for conflict. You need not confine your thoughts to our recent experiences; read *Wall Street Under Oath*,[2] about congres-

---

[2] Ferdinand Pecora, *Wall Street Under Oath* (New York: Simon & Schuster, 1936).

sional hearings that followed the 1929 stock market crash. The story repeats itself.

Those who choose to link origination and distribution in investment banks should be required to certify that the CEO and other designated senior managers on both sides of the potential conflict have responsibility for maintaining appropriate separations. Moreover, we should treat failures to properly supervise as (a) *personal* and (b) *criminal*, as is currently our practice with price fixing. I believe that the conflict can be extinguished with appropriate disciplines.

AUDITORS, LAWYERS, AND PROFESSIONALS

For many of us who have operated in the business world over the last forty years, it has been clear that there has been a gradual but continual movement away from standards and values, toward processes and procedures. Where we used to look to accountants to help us properly account for a transaction, we now look to them to verify that it "complies with GAAP." There is a big difference. The same is true with the law, moving from "Is it right?" to "Can it be defended?" What used to be part of an immune system has become too close to being part of operating management. There are many explanations for this change and the relationship cannot be legislated to return to a world that was probably never perfect. However, the value and need for true professionalism must be reaffirmed.

More broadly, corporate America must reaffirm a commitment to basic values if our system of capitalism is to regain the public's trust.

Chapter 3

Management as a Profession

**RAKESH KHURANA, NITIN NOHRIA,
AND DANIEL PENRICE**

Repeated and, as of this writing, ongoing revelations of corporate wrongdoing over the past two years have eroded public trust in business institutions and executives to levels not seen in decades. A recent Gallup poll indicates that Americans now have no more trust in business leaders than they do in Washington politicians.[1] Fairly or not, people have become willing to believe that executives, as a class, are greedy and dishonest.

However natural it might be to ask how so many executives—not to mention accountants, investment bankers, stock market analysts, lawyers, money managers, and others implicated in recent acts of corporate malfeasance—could have become so depraved, this is probably the wrong question. Given that human nature does not change much from age to age, the real issue is the effectiveness of the constraints that society places on the purely selfish impulses of individuals. In response to the recent scandals, politicians and government officials have stepped in to pass new laws and create new regulations, while

Please direct all correspondence to Rakesh Khurana, Harvard Business School, Morgan Hall 329, Boston MA 02163. The authors gratefully acknowledge generous support from the Harvard Business School Division of Research and Faculty Development and a research grant from the John F. Kennedy School of Government's Center for Public Leadership.

[1] Joseph Carroll, Gallup Organization Poll Analysis: Gallup's Annual Survey on the Honesty and Ethics of Various Professions, December 1, 2003.

prominent persons on Wall Street and elsewhere in the business community have issued their own calls for reform in such areas as accounting practices and executive compensation. Yet while laws, regulations, and policies have a clear role to play here, they are a relatively expensive and inefficient way for a society to promote responsible conduct and trustworthy business leadership.

In the case of bad behavior on the part of business executives, the reason that the issue of trust arises is that these individuals are expected to exercise judgment—based on specialized knowledge and methods of analysis that they alone are thought to possess—in areas in which their decisions affect the well-being of others. When the need for such judgment has arisen in other spheres that are vital to the interests of society (such as law and government, military affairs, health, and religion, to consider the classic examples), modern societies have responded by creating the institutions that we know as professions. One way of diagnosing the cause of the recent epidemic of business scandals would be to speak of a widespread failure among CEOs and other senior executives (along with board members, auditors, financial analysts, and others) to uphold their professional obligations.

▶ *In comparing management with the more traditional professions of law and medicine one inevitably finds it wanting. This shortcoming has a direct bearing on society's ability to demand and obtain responsible conduct from executives, as well as on management's ability to maintain the public trust required for the optimal functioning of our economic institutions.*

To speak of the professional obligations of individuals such as CEOs and other executives is to imply that business management itself is a profession—but is it? Sociologists who study the professions have employed a wide range of perspectives and criteria for determining what makes an occupation a profession. For the purposes of our present inquiry, we have chosen four traits and practices out of the network of those that have been found to be associated with professions. We use these traits and practices both to set forth our own notion of the essence of professionalism and to enable us to compare management with what we take to be the bona fide professions, in particular law and medicine.[2] Our criteria for calling an occupation a bona fide profession are as follows:

- a common body of knowledge resting on a well-developed, widely accepted theoretical base;

- a system for certifying that individuals possess such knowledge before being licensed or otherwise allowed to practice;

- a commitment to use specialized knowledge for the public good, and a renunciation of the goal of profit maximization, in return for professional autonomy and monopoly power;

- a code of ethics, with provisions for monitoring individual compliance with the code and a system of sanctions for enforcing it.

In comparing management with the more traditional professions of law and medicine along these criteria, one inevitably finds it wanting.[3] (We say this despite the inroads made by market values at the expense of traditionally professional ones that have been observable in both law and medicine in recent years.) This shortcoming, we believe, has a direct bearing on society's

---

[2] Our definition, choice of criteria, and analysis of professions draw extensively on Everett Cherrington Hughes, *Men and Their Work* (Glencoe, IL: Free Press, 1958); Andrew Abbott, *The System of Professions: An Essay on the Division of Expert Labor* (Chicago: University of Chicago Press, 1988); and Eliot Freidson, *Professionalism: The Third Logic* (Chicago: University of Chicago Press, 2001). These three scholars have been the most influential analysts of the professions in recent decades, and though readers will find several specific references to their works in this essay, their fundamental ways of thinking about professions have profoundly influenced our own. Hughes constructs professions around the identity of those practicing a particular occupation. Abbott analyzes the process by which occupations gain, maintain, adjust, and sometimes lose their ability to control particular tasks in competition with other occupations. Freidson describes professions as institutional systems that stand apart from the logic of the market.

[3] For an excellent sociological review of the development of the medical profession, see Paul Starr, *The Social Transformation of American Medicine* (New York: Basic Books, 1982). For an overview of the emergence of the modern legal profession, see Paul A. Freund, "The Legal Profession," in Kenneth Lynn, ed., *The Professions in America* (New York: Houghton Mifflin, 1965), 35–46; see also L. C. B. Gower and Leolin Price, "The Profession and Practice of the Law in England and America," *Modern Law Review* 20 (July 1957): 317.

ability to demand and obtain responsible conduct from executives, as well as on management's ability to maintain the public trust required for the optimal functioning of our economic institutions. While not intending to idealize what we have called the bona fide professions, we believe that the comparison we undertake in this paper has merit as a way of suggesting how management as an institution might be reformed, other than through the blunt instruments of law and regulation on the one hand and well-meaning but ultimately toothless calls for greater individual integrity and ethics on the other.

The sociology of the professions is too large a body of theoretical and empirical analysis to be more than sketched in this paper. It is also a field that has not yet taken management as a central subject of empirical study. We shall therefore deal only with some of the central problems of the structure of management. Even then, for lack of space, our objective in this essay is not to make an airtight case about the state of contemporary management, but rather to raise important questions. By comparing management with the legal and medical professions, we hope to stimulate discussion and debate that can lead to a deeper understanding of the current state of management.[4]

We have listed four criteria for determining whether management can be considered a genuine profession. Let us consider how management in its present institutional state matches up against each of these criteria.

[4] We recognize that the occupational category of management includes as heterogeneous a group as exists within any of the occupations in our society. The general title "manager" says little about the person who holds the position. As Abbott (1988) notes, a manager may have a high-school education, an undergraduate degree, a master's degree, or a doctorate. He or she may be an administrator in a large corporation or an entrepreneur. Because the diversity among business managers is as great as the variety of types of business in the United States, the risks of generalizing about managers as a class are clear and problematic—but an essay that seeks to interpret and analyze the situation of an occupation must be more than an account of its variety. That said, when we refer to management in this paper, we start with Erik Olin Wright's definition, in *Class Counts* (Cambridge, UK: Cambridge University Press, 1997) of managers as principally salaried employees of an organization who perform tasks involving the coordination of the labor of others, in positions requiring at minimum a four-year college degree, and with general knowledge of one or more business functions. We then expand this definition to those who provide services in such fields as investment banking and consulting.

COMMON BODY OF KNOWLEDGE RESTING ON WELL-DEVELOPED, WIDELY ACCEPTED THEORETICAL BASE

The traditional professions of law, medicine, and the clergy all have deep historical roots in another major institution of Western society: the university. Roman and canon law, medicine, and theology, in fact, constituted three of the four faculties of the medieval European university, and they survive to this day—in schools of law, medicine, and divinity, respectively—in the modern American university. The study of law in America today remains rooted in the centuries-old traditions of Roman and Anglo-American law, as systematized and interpreted by the discipline of legal philosophy, or jurisprudence. Law students now learn the law not as a collection of statutes but rather as a set of principles, doctrines, and rules that have evolved over the course of centuries and are said to constitute legal reasoning itself. The study of medicine, for its part, has been continually transformed since the Middle Ages by the rise and ongoing progress of modern science. The development of the germ theory of disease in the nineteenth century, for example, and of the science of genetics in the twentieth, have gone into the formation of a theoretical structure that undergirds the body of knowledge every medical student is now required to master. The medical school curriculum proceeds from the premise that in order to diagnose and treat disease, the would-be physician must have a firm grounding in what science (or, perhaps more accurately, what is generally accepted as science) currently understands to be its causes.

Turning to the body of systematized knowledge underpinning the claim that business management too is a profession, we find important differences between management as a science and the knowledge bases of the traditional professions. It is not just that the study of management was a latecomer to the university—which, since the creation of the modern American research university in the last three decades of the nineteenth century, has gained an effective monopoly on professional education[5] (the

[5] For an account of how this process occurred, see Laurence R. Veysey, *The Emergence of the American University* (Chicago: University of Chicago Press, 1965).

first university-based business school in America, the University of Pennsylvania's Wharton School of Finance, was not founded until 1881[6]). For even as management was being gingerly accepted as a subject deserving of inclusion within the university, the discipline of management—following close behind the occupation itself—was having to be invented *ex nihilo*. The professionalization of management, which was what business schools were founded to undertake, began as a quest to delve beneath the practice of business, with its rule-of-thumb approach to business problems, to discover a set of underlying principles that could explain effective practice. These basic principles were by no means evident to the pioneers of academic business education—and, as we suggest, they remain by no means evident today.[7]

During the time that the first business schools were being constituted, at the beginning of the twentieth century, "scientific management" was in the air, as Frederick Taylor's application of scientific methods to the study of physical labor had begun to be extended to the organization of industry as well as to spheres such as higher education and government.[8] While Taylorism was

[6] For a history of the founding of the Wharton School at the University of Pennsylvania, see Steven A. Sass, *The Pragmatic Imagination: A History of the Wharton School, 1881–1981* (Philadelphia: University of Pennsylvania Press, 1982).

[7] There is an opposing argument to the effect that while business education may be messier and less well-grounded in a firm or coherent knowledge base than legal or medical education, that messiness might be closer to the realities of its practitioners' actual experiences than are the formalities of legal and medical education to the realities of their practitioners' experiences. (For an example of this approach to conceptualizing professional knowledge, see Donald A. Schon, *The Reflective Practitioner* (New York: Basic Books, 1983.) Consequently, despite what they were taught in medical school (the systems of the body; the base disciplines of biology, chemistry, and physics) or law school (torts, contracts, constitutional law), many medical and legal practitioners will contend that they learned to be doctors or lawyers not in the classroom but in rotations and residencies, or in writing contracts, negotiating settlements, and arguing cases, respectively. Like Abbott (1988), we believe that this view confounds two dimensions of professional education: explicit knowledge and implicit knowledge, the latter of which can be learned only through direct experience. It was not until medical and legal education could successfully claim the importance of theoretical, abstract knowledge that entry into these occupations moved away from the guild and apprenticeship model (Starr, 1982). For our purposes, we would like to separate these two dimensions of professional education and concentrate on explicit knowledge.

[8] Steven R. Barley and Gideon Kunda, "Design and Devotion: Surges of Rational and Normative Ideologies of Control in Managerial Discourse," *Administrative Science Quarterly* 33 (September 1992): 24–60.

quickly jettisoned as the core of the business school curriculum, it made scientific reasoning and method appear to be applicable to business, thus helping to legitimate the study of business as an activity within the university. Yet what exactly a "science" of management should study would be puzzled over and debated for a great many years. Three curricular models emerged and competed with one another in the early decades of university business education. The first was a simple aggregation of courses taught elsewhere in the university and covering such obviously useful (if intellectually circumscribed) subjects as accounting and business law. The second model attempted to organize business education around specific industries such as banking, transportation, merchandising, mining, and lumber. The third model—increasingly adopted by the 1930s, and still the basis of the business school curriculum today—was the functional approach, as the grouping of courses began to mirror the differentiation of

▶ *The professionalization of management, which was what business schools were founded to undertake, began as a quest to delve beneath the practice of business, with its rule-of-thumb approach to business problems, to discover a set of underlying principles that could explain effective practice.*

finance, administration, operations, and marketing as the major activities of the firm. Thus, the curricular structure evolved as a pragmatic response to the challenge of turning out graduates who could perform the tasks that would be required of them by employers.[9]

It is not that no attempts were made, in the meantime, to discover an underlying general theory that would inform the tasks of a manager. But the search for a theoretical model capable of explaining effective business practice—which was actually a search for an existing discipline or set of disciplines from which such a model could be produced—foundered for many years on disagreements about the nature of business firms and

[9] For a description of the early business curricula, see Willard E. Hotchkiss, "The Basic Elements and Their Proper Balance in the Curriculum of a Collegiate Business School," *Journal of Political Economy* 28 (February 1920): 89–107; see also Edward Jones, "Some Propositions Concerning University Instruction in Business Administration," *Journal of Political Economy* 21 (March 1913): 185–95.

the ultimate purpose of business. The decision (made very early in the history of university-based business education) to remove the study of business from economics departments stemmed from the recognition that economics, at the time, had no interest in one of management's most pressing concerns—namely, the internal organization of the firm. When experimentation with various disciplines—including sociology, psychology, and even (at Harvard Business School's Fatigue Laboratory, from the 1920s to the 1940s) physiology—yielded results that were either too politically radical for the university's guardians and patrons (as happened at the Wharton School during the Progressive Era) or simply lacking in explanatory power and practical applicability, the resulting void at the center of the business school curriculum eventually caused business educators to take a second look at the discipline of economics.

Economics, in the decades prior to World War II, had occupied a relatively weak position in the disciplinary pecking order. Yet as the growing acceptance of Keynesian theory in the postwar years gave the subject greater prestige, and the 1958 reports on the state of business education in America by the Carnegie Corporation and the Ford Foundation led to a greater emphasis on the social sciences and quantitative method in business schools,[10] economics began to move into the position of dominance that it enjoys in the MBA curriculum today. Building on the foundational work of Adolf Berle and Gardiner Means on the separation of ownership and control in the large corporation, and of Ronald Coase on the significance of transaction costs, economists such as Michael Jensen and Oliver Williamson began, in the 1970s, to develop a new theory of the firm that treated it not as a "black box" that converted inputs into outputs but rather as an institution requiring and rewarding economic analysis.[11] It is undeniable that these and other recent economic

[10] For the Carnegie report, see Frank Pierson, *The Education of American Businessmen* (New York: McGraw Hill, 1959). For the Ford report, see Robert Aaron Gordon and James E. Howell, *Higher Education for Business* (New York: Columbia University Press, 1959).

[11] The foundational paper for agency theory—one of the most influential contributions from the discipline of economics to a theory of the firm—is Michael C. Jensen

theorists have contributed important insights into the internal workings of firms that are applicable to managerial practice. Yet they have also left business education with a dominant theory that, in adhering to many of the individualist assumptions and methodologies of neoclassical economics, is unable to account for much of the social environment of business—including the social and cultural factors that make themselves felt within organizations, as well as other essential aspects of the phenomenon that it purports to explain.[12]

SYSTEM OF CERTIFICATION

Besides having failed to develop a body of knowledge and theory comparable to those of the true professions, management differs from these other occupations in lacking a set of institutions designed to certify that its practitioners have a basic mastery of a core body of specialized knowledge and can apply it judiciously. In medicine and law, for example, there are institutions that specify the educational requirements (i.e., the MD or JD degree) that anyone desirous of practicing the profession must obtain. Beyond these educational requirements, aspirants to membership in these and other recognized professions must obtain a license to practice by passing a comprehensive exam designed to test mastery of the knowledge ostensibly acquired in professional school. Once the aspiring professional passes that exam, he or she must invest in a certain amount of continuing education in order to stay abreast of evolving knowledge in the profession and to maintain a license to practice.

and William H. Meckling, "Theory of the Firm: Managerial Behavior, Agency Costs, and Ownership Structure," *Journal of Financial Economics* 3 (April 1976): 305–60. For the outlines of transaction cost theory, see Oliver E. Williamson, *Markets and Hierarchies: Analysis and Antitrust Implications* (New York: Free Press, 1975).
[12] For critiques of relying on economic theory to inform managerial education, see Sumantra Ghoshal and Peter Moran, "Bad for Practice: A Critique of Transaction Cost Theory," *Academy of Management Review* 21 (January 1996): 13-47; Jeffrey Pfeffer, *New Directions for Organization Theory: Problems and Prospects* (New York: Oxford University Press, 1997); and Fabrizio Ferraro, Jeffrey Pfeffer, and Robert I. Sutton, "Economics Language and Assumptions: How Theories Can Become Self-Fulfilling," *Academy of Management Review* (forthcoming).

Management differs from medicine, law, and other recognized professions in having neither a formal educational requirement nor a system of examination and licensing for aspiring members. Although the MBA has been the fastest-growing graduate degree for the past twenty years, it is not a requirement for becoming a manager.[13] It is true that for those seeking access to senior executive positions or work in the fields of investment banking or consulting, an MBA has become a de facto requirement. Yet even in these cases, there is no requirement of passing a standard exam before being admitted to practice, nor are senior managers, investment bankers, or consultants required to participate in continuing education. There is no explicit obligation, for example, for experienced, high-level managers to know anything about investing in innovative new financial derivatives or special-purpose vehicles, even if they serve on boards that are required to approve such potentially risky transactions. In fact, data on enrollment in executive education programs offered by business schools suggest that those who already possess an MBA are the least likely to pursue continuing education.[14]

▶ *Besides having failed to develop a body of knowledge and theory comparable to those of the true professions, management differs from these other occupations in lacking a set of institutions designed to certify that its practitioners have a basic mastery of a core body of specialized knowledge and can apply it judiciously.*

How would having a formal educational requirement and a system of certification and mandatory continuing education advance the practice of management? Although such barriers to entry would have the effect of closing managerial positions to some who now aspire to them, all true professions are, almost by definition, closed systems that tightly control and carefully restrict access to their ranks. Closure in professions need not, as some might fear in the case of management, stifle innovation and progress. In the field of medicine, for example, the pace of

---

[13] Jeffrey Pfeffer and Christina T. Fong, "The End of Business Schools? Less Success than Meets the Eye," *Academy of Management Learning and Education* 1 (2002): 78–95.

[14] Walter Kiechel, Presentation on trends in business press publishing and executive education to Harvard Business School faculty, Fall, 2002.

discovery and creative progress rapidly accelerated in the wake of professionalization. In an open society, moreover, there will always be room for "rogue" entrepreneurs to challenge the existing order, as practitioners of alternative medicine are challenging the medical profession today. Meanwhile, from society's point of view, meanwhile, professional closure offers distinct benefits when the privilege of closure is granted in return for the commitments that true professionals make to serve the public good and to forgo certain forms of self-interested behavior.

COMMITMENT TO SPECIALIZED KNOWLEDGE AS A PUBLIC GOOD; RENUNCIATION OF PROFIT MAXIMIZATION

To be able to set and enforce standards of admission to a profession, determine how professional work is to be done, engage in self-regulation rather than be subjected to extensive regulation from without, and reap the economic benefits of a monopoly position in the marketplace—these are all privileges that society grants to professions in return for certain social benefits. The creation of these social benefits, in turn, places certain constraints on professionals. Because they possess specialized knowledge in areas of vital concern to society, genuine professionals are expected to place that knowledge at the disposal of all who require it and to provide services in a way that places the maintenance of professional standards and values ahead of the securing of individual advantage. The renunciation of unabashed self-interest that society expects of true professionals takes a very particular form: unlike actors in the marketplace, as envisioned by classical and neoclassical economics, professionals engage in work out of more than merely economic motives, and they eschew profit maximization (as opposed to profit making) as a goal.[15] Indeed, because of the exemption they have been granted

[15] In a recent interview, Harvard University president Lawrence Summers noted that one should not confound private gain with societal contribution when examining the value of professions: "Where our professional schools are concerned, I think we all are convinced that the value of an activity or a profession is not measured by how large a house its practitioners live in" ("The President's Perspective," *Harvard Magazine*, January–February 2004, 52).

from certain laws of market exchange, professionals are specifically enjoined from using the laws of the market to reap economic gain at the expense of their professional obligations.

Implicit in this aspect of professionalism is the idea that, even
when serving private clients, professionals are providing a public
good. In economics, the provision of public goods has been
widely recognized as a case that creates exceptions to the rules
governing the provision of goods for purely private consumption. Lawyers serve private clients (be they individuals, corporations, or other private entities) but are understood to be providing a public good—if not justice in every case, then at least the
implementation of the rule of law. Likewise, physicians serve private individuals but are understood, in so doing, to be providing
the public good of health for
the general population. That
the advocacy system in
American jurisprudence or
the structure of the health-
care market in the United
States (with its convoluted
system of both private and
public third-party payers) can
tempt lawyers and doctors,
respectively, to lose sight of professional obligations beyond
serving the interests of particular clients does not invalidate this
more general truth. Once a professional loses sight of the larger
social benefit that his or her work is intended to provide, the
line between professional services and commerce becomes dan-
gerously blurred.

> *The notion that those who lead and
manage our society's major private economic
institutions might provide, or be responsible for
providing, a public good is quite foreign to our
customary way of thinking about management. Yet this idea was often voiced by those
who led American business schools in the early
decades of their existence.*

The notion that those who lead and manage our society's
major private economic institutions might provide, or be
responsible for providing, a public good is quite foreign to our
customary way of thinking about management. Yet this idea was
often voiced by those who led American business schools in the
early decades of their existence. For example, in a speech titled
"The Social Significance of Business," delivered at Stanford
University's School of Business shortly after its founding in 1925

(and subsequently published as an article in the *Harvard Business Review*), Wallace B. Donham, the second dean of Harvard Business School, declared that the "development, strengthening, and multiplication of socially minded business men is the central problem of business." As Donham went on to say:

> The socializing of industry from within on a higher ethical plane, not socialism nor communism, not government operation nor the exercise of the police power, but rather the development from within the business group of effective social control of those mechanisms which have been placed in the hands of the race through all the recent extraordinary revolutionizing of material things, is greatly needed. The business group largely controls these mechanisms and is therefore in a strategic position to solve these problems. Our objective therefore, should be the multiplication of men who will handle their current business problems in socially constructive ways.[16]

Haunted by a belief that scientific, technological, and material progress was outstripping society's capacity for moral self-governance, and that the professions that had traditionally provided social and moral leadership (i.e., law and the clergy) were no longer up to the task, Donham looked to a new "profession of business" for nothing less than saving modern, industrial civilization from itself. As the professionalization project that had provided the agenda for American business education from its founding up until the outbreak of World War II was abandoned in the postwar decades, expectations of what managers should contribute to society became rather more modest, to say the least.

Today, in place of such notions as the "socializing of industry from within" and the concept of the business executive as an expert capable of, and responsible for, solving some of the most urgent problems facing modern societies, we find American business schools propagating the doctrine of shareholder primacy and the paradigm of the manager as the mere agent of the

---

[16] Wallace B. Donham, "The Social Significance of Business," reprinted from *Harvard Business Review* (July 1927) in the printed document *Dedication Addresses*, Harvard Business School Archives Collection (AC 1927 17.1).

company's "owners". Taken in combination, these two concepts—both outgrowths of the intellectual domination of American business education by economics during the past three decades—make managers anything but disinterested experts oriented toward the needs of society that we take to be part of the essence of professionalism. The doctrine of shareholder primacy has legitimized the idea that the benefits of managerial expertise may be offered for purely private gain and that this is equivalent to advancing societal interests. Having given rise to the notion of making managers "think and behave like owners" through equity-linked compensation, agency theory can now be seen to have led directly to many of the worst profit-maximizing abuses unmasked in the recent wave of corporate scandals.[17]

Now that the traditional professions have come under attack for providing refuge from the disciplining forces of the market, it is worth noting that a great many American business leaders who have enriched themselves spectacularly in recent years without engaging in actual malfeasance have managed to do so by insulating themselves from such fundamental market imperatives as "pay for performance"—meanwhile declining to accept the constraints that prevent legitimate professionals from engaging in profit maximization. If the traditional professions are to be asked to accept a greater role for market forces, is it too much to ask businesspersons who enjoy exemptions from market discipline to accept a greater role for professionalism?[18]

▶ *If the traditional professions are to be asked to accept a greater role for market forces, is it too much to ask businesspersons who enjoy exemptions from market discipline to accept a greater role for professionalism?*

[17] In the wake of the corporate scandals and the burst of the stock market bubble, Michael Jensen has retreated from his unconditional support for stock options, which he now describes as "managerial heroin." However, he continues to dismiss the view that managers and corporations should be concerned with any constituency other than shareholders. See Jeff Madrick, "Are Corporate Scandals Just Greed, or a Predictable Result of a Theory?" *New York Times*, February 20, 2003. Jensen's view can be described as the University of Chicago perspective, in which maximizing shareholder value is seen as tantamount to a public service.

[18] While addressing the critique of professions that points to their relative insulation from market forces, it is worth noting that those who advocate the economic logic of

CODE OF ETHICS

The fourth and final dimension on which, in our view, management differs significantly from the true professions is that its members are not governed by a shared normative code that is reinforced by institutions that promote adherence to it. Such a normative code, whether known as a code of ethics or a code of conduct, is a central feature of almost any occupational group that desires to be seen as a profession. Though normative codes exist among "professions" as diverse as librarianship and plumbing, the true professions go farther than simply having a written code by which members are encouraged to abide voluntarily. They teach the meaning and consequences of the code as a part of the formal education of their members. They test and verify this understanding through licensing exams. Once licensed, members are required to adhere to the code in order to maintain a license. A governing body, composed of respected members of the profession, oversees adherence to the code by establishing monitoring mechanisms, reviewing complaints, and administering sanctions—including the ultimate sanction of revoking an individual's license to operate as a professional.

the market or the benefits of bureaucracy often treat professions as an aberration rather than something with an institutional logic of their own. As Freidson (2001) has persuasively argued, unless the institutional logic of professions and professionalism is understood and granted equal standing with that of the market or the firm, competition and regulatory control will continue to erode professional autonomy and, ultimately, the quality of professional work. (For example, see Felix Rohatyn, "The Financial Scandals and the Demise of the Traditional Investment Banker" and Geneva Overholser, "Journalists and the Corporate Scandals: What Happened to the Watchdog?" in this volume). What we are arguing for is the need for ongoing tension between the laws of the market and professional obligations. The two can coexist—and must necessarily do so—in our society. Yet even though both are given scope to operate in the other occupations (with market forces gaining increasing strength in law and medicine in recent years), professional obligations seem not to be a factor in management. It is when we mistakenly believe that market forces can perform the same function as professional obligations, or that they provide a superior logic that obviates the need for professional obligations, that occupational domains get into trouble. As C. Wright Mills noted in *White Collar* (New York: Oxford University Press, 1951), American business is animated by individualism, both in ideology and in practice. The professions, by contrast, have a concern with the community's interests, which is a different institutional logic. Consequently, many social scientists have believed that the process by which individual and societal interests can be aligned is through the professionalization of business. The sociologist

Professions establish these codes, and the institutions to enforce them, as part of their implicit contract with society. "Trust us to exercise jurisdiction over an important occupational category," these professions essentially state. "In return, we will make every effort to ensure that the members of our profession are worthy of your trust, that they will not only be competent to perform the tasks with which they have been entrusted but will also adhere to high standards and conduct themselves with integrity." The privilege of self-regulation is granted out of society's recognition that in cases involving the use of highly specialized knowledge, laypersons may not be in a position to pass accurate and fair judgment on the conduct of specialists.

Most normative codes, like the ancient Hippocratic Oath for doctors, clearly articulate a profession's higher aims and social purposes and the manner in which these purposes must be pursued. Such role definitions have many benefits; one is that by establishing a normative standard for inclusion, they create and sustain a sense of community and mutual obligation among the members of a profession, as well as a sense of obligation to the profession as an abstract social entity. These bonds of membership create the social capital of a profession, which builds trust and significantly reduces transaction costs among members of that profession and between the profession and society. As we observed at the beginning of this paper, trust in management as

Emile Durkheim, for example, in *Professional Ethics and Civic Morals* (London: Routledge and Kegan Paul, 1957), made the point that "There are professional ethics for the priest, the lawyer, the magistrate. . . . Why should there not be one for trade and industry?" (29). Similarly, the social commentator Walter Lippmann, in *Drift and Mastery* (Madison, WI: University of Wisconsin Press, 1961), argued that a well-functioning society exists where individual and community interests are aligned. He welcomed the development of graduate schools of business administration in the early twentieth century, describing it as an opportunity for business leadership to pass into "the hands of men interested in production as a creative art instead of as brute exploitation" (44) and for business to become "a profession with university standing equal to that of law, medicine, or engineering" (43). Louis D. Brandeis similarly maintained that through the professionalization of management, business would become aligned with the interests of democratic society; see *Business: A Profession* (Boston: Hale, Cushman, & Flint, 1933), 12.

Besides the inevitable and potentially fruitful tension between market forces and professional obligations, one must also consider the inevitable tension between professionals and organizations. As we have noted in this paper, one of the essential an institution could not be much lower than it is in American society today. In light of that, the benefits of a true profession of management adopting a formal normative code would appear to be obvious—particularly in comparison with a regulatory regime that could all too easily stifle the innovation and risk taking that have contributed so much to the success of American capitalism.

Legal and regulatory overreaction to the crisis currently afflicting American business and management, however, is only one of the dangers that we now face. Another danger is that business education and its supporting institution of management—in heeding the cries for integrity and ethics that have gone up on all sides in the wake of the recent corporate scandals—will succeed in allaying the public's skepticism through such measures as new ethics curricula and corporate ethical codes (Enron famously possessed one of the latter while its top managers were busy destroying the wealth of their shareholders and the livelihoods of their employees) that merely create an appearance of reform without delivering the genuine article. As we have recently learned from such phenomena as the weak link between executive compensation and firm performance, and the impotence of so many corporate boards, American managers have become quite adept at decoupling the formal structures and symbols of their "professionalism"—those features that give them legitimacy in the eyes of the public—from their actual work activities.[19]

---

attributes of professions is autonomy and self-regulation. Yet when professionals perform their work in the context of formal organizations premised on the coordination of a variety of activities by means of authority, conflict necessarily arises. (See Kevin Leicht and Mary Fennell's *Professional Work: A Sociological Approach* [Malden, MA: Blackwell Publishers, 2001] and William T. Allen and Geoffrey Miller's "Professional Independence and the Corporate Lawyer," in this volume.) Just as market forces and professional obligations must coexist within professions, it is necessary to find some compromise, within organizations employing professionals, between professional roles and organizational necessities, lest such organizations lose either their effectiveness or their sense of purpose.

[19] To be fair, there is little doubt that the lawyers and accountants who aided Enron successfully decoupled the features of legal and auditing professionalism, respectively, from their actual work. How organizational processes successfully decouple formal structures from actual activities is summarized in Paul J. Dimaggio and Walter W. Powell, "The Iron Cage Revisited: Institutional Isomorphism and Collective Rationality in Organizational Fields," *American Sociological Review* 48 (1983): 147–160.

Our speculations about a genuine professionalization of management as a remedy for the crisis of legitimacy now facing American business may strike some as radical. But assuming, once again, that increased regulation is not the whole or the best answer to the problem at hand, we believe that our idea of making management into a bona fide profession has the virtue of asking a group that has seriously abused the public's trust to make a serious commitment to restoring it.

One way of looking at the problem with American management today, we would argue, is that it has succeeded in assuming many of the appearances and privileges of professionalism while evading the attendant constraints and responsibilities. Although it is now fashionable in some quarters, as we have suggested, to denigrate professionals as elites enjoying shelter from the rough-and-tumble of the marketplace, do we as a society really wish to surrender the benefits that we rightfully demand of professionals in return? And given the inevitable existence of elite knowledge workers, such as managers, in complex modern societies, ought we not to be concerned with producing elites who are motivated by something beyond the pursuit of self-interest under the laws of the marketplace, or the fear of punishment under the laws of the land? A self-interested, self-indulgent corporate leadership is not inevitable, and a model for something better lies at hand. We can find it in the flawed but durable institutions that serve society by meriting the label "profession."

PART II

Reimagining Gatekeeper Identities

Chapter 4

The Regulators and the Financial Scandals

DONALD C. LANGEVOORT

A matrix of possibilities confronts any effort to evaluate the regulators' role in the recent financial scandals. There are the various minimally coordinated sources of regulation: Congress, the Securities and Exchange Commission, the states (for both corporation law and state blue sky law), the stock exchanges, and the judiciary. Then there is the temporal dimension: each of these sources has performed differently before the scandals erupted, during the perceived crisis, and now, in a somewhat quieter period, as political attention has shifted away from the obsession with corporate wrongdoing.

Compounding the analytical challenge is the fact that we do not yet fully understand the causes of the observed symptoms of distress, or even the severity of the illness. Although there has certainly been a run of notorious scandals and a marked increase in accounting restatements in the past few years, the percentage of issuers caught up in allegations of wrongdoing remains relatively small compared with the universe of listed companies. Perhaps this is just the usual hangover from the end of a bull market, different in intensity only because the bull market binge was so sustained.

All this counsels a fair amount of caution in any commentary. But I will venture a guess that in the 1990s we did see a "norms

Some of the thoughts expressed in this essay are developed more fully in "Managing the 'Expectations Gap' in Investor Protection: The SEC and the Post-Enron Reform Agenda," *Villanova Law Review* 48 (2003): 1139.

shift" in the philosophy toward financial reporting—a shift that provoked some to excesses that constituted criminal misconduct. There is now, among corporate and securities scholars, a fairly standard explanation of what happened. First, changes in the form of executive compensation created a managerial bias toward high stock prices that gradually turned into an obsession, especially pronounced at times when lock-up and holding periods expired. The investing public, gradually showing more exuberance and less critical discipline, demanded metrics in financial reporting, showing sustained and rapid growth to justify the stock price increases, which managers delivered. The institutions that were expected to provide a check on bias and cheating—auditors especially, but also outside directors, lawyers, and securities analysts—failed in their monitoring and gatekeeping responsibilities, partly because conflicting interests compromised their independence and partly because no one wanted responsibility for reducing shareholder wealth by popping the stock price bubble that was making nearly everyone richer.

▶ *It was a "can do" culture gone awry. The only surprise was that neither directors nor investors realized that consistently meeting such aggressive targets should raise a red flag in the corporation's internal controls system rather than prompt a celebratory round of options, bonuses, and further inflation of the stock price.*

Without doubting the rough accuracy of the standard account, I suspect that the story is more complicated in at least two respects. Ironically, some of the dysfunction may have come about precisely because of improvements in corporate governance and efficiency-promoting mechanisms. In an increasingly hypercompetitive global marketplace, boards of directors (under pressure from sophisticated investors with a short-term focus) placed extraordinary performance demands on CEOs for top- and bottom-line growth. As a result, anyone wanting to be chosen as a CEO had to demonstrate unabashed confidence in, and commitment to, the ability to make high numbers. This created what economists describe as a "last period" incentive on the part of the chosen to overpromise, take the lucrative compensation in the interim, and engage in increasingly aggressive efforts to delay, if not gamble out from, any day of reckoning. Much of the resulting responsibility was pushed down the organization, so that subordinates (often under the direction of the chief financial officer) had to invent ways of meeting nearly impossible demands. It was a "can do" culture gone awry. The only surprise was that neither directors nor investors realized that consistently meeting such aggressive targets should raise a red flag in the corporation's internal controls system[1] rather than prompt a celebratory round of options, bonuses, and further inflation of the stock price.

The other part of the story has to do with financial innovation—especially in derivatives, structured finance, and other forms of synthetic finance—and involves parallel tracks in both financial reporting and tax avoidance. Technology permitted rapid innovation, and the markets rewarded it. But the pace of change destabilized the underlying norms of financial reporting: How were these complex developments to be accounted for fairly? Legitimately difficult problems arose, and the system had neither the time nor the incentive to answer them carefully. As a result, the answers were created "on the fly," which inevitably meant they had a self-serving bias. Temporary and inadequate responses (such as the 3 percent equity rule for off-books treatment of special-purpose financing entities) became embedded in practice. Gradually, the destabilization of financial reporting norms became such that—for many executives in the 1990s—the very system of financial reporting seemed archaic and artificial. That in turn made it easy for those executives to rationalize a jettisoning of the principle of conservatism on which accounting is founded. The loss of restraint started some on a mindless slide down a slippery slope, past the point where aggressiveness becomes fraud. Others, seeing no real market or legal penalties for pervasive aggressiveness, persuaded themselves that they could engineer cleverly deceitful practices and just not be caught.

[1] See William Beaver, "What Have We Learned from the Recent Corporate Scandals That We Did Not Already Know?" *Stanford Journal of Law, Business, and Finance* 8 (2002): 155, 163.

How much of this norms shift was the regulators' fault? For simplicity, let me focus here simply on federal securities regulation. As a structural matter, our system of securities regulation does not seek more than minimal *ex ante* regulatory control over disclosure. Outside the initial public offering (IPO) context, at least, SEC "real time" review of disclosure is episodic and fairly superficial. The real work is left to the private gatekeepers, with the SEC's main focus being *ex post* enforcement as a deterrent. The SEC's budget, resources, and morale are overwhelmed by rapid growth in the markets. Its resources have never been adequate for any deep policing of managerial misbehavior, and they have become more grossly inadequate over time. Moreover, SEC enforcement proceedings have long been selective and frequently have been settled on terms that made the risk taken in violating the law worthwhile. Hence, the deterrence effect was inadequate. But the Commission cannot be blamed for what it was not given—only, perhaps, for not being candid about its relative impotence.

Perhaps the SEC can be faulted for not contesting more aggressively the devolution of financial reporting norms through rule making or interpretation. Here again, however, limited resources made this difficult, and the pace of innovation was so rapid that any systematic intervention would probably have been obsolete before completion. In cases such as the expensing of stock option grants, in which the SEC was initially inclined to intervene, it met substantial political resistance from the branches of government on which it depended for its ever-thinning resources. The success of that political pressure not only provided cover for further devolution but also encouraged even more rationalization of misreporting: If the government was not all that serious about high-quality financial reporting, why should executives be?

If the foregoing account is roughly right, then the responses we have seen from Congress and the SEC in the aftermath of the scandals are on the mark. I will leave to others a discussion of the specific reforms addressed to the various gatekeepers, such as the creation of the Public Company Accounting Oversight

Board and the lawyers' new reporting obligations (both of which I like) or the new director independence requirements (about which I am more ambivalent). To me, the most important reform in the Sarbanes-Oxley Act of 2002 was actually the budget increase given to the SEC, which allows for the rebuilding of staff resources, expertise, and morale so badly depleted in the preceding decade. This creates at least the possibility of restoring within the agency a professional culture that, among other things, attracts people with a deep commitment to its mission. Though it is still not enough to permit the level of policing of financial reporting needed for total investor confidence in the face of strong managerial temptations to cheat, it will help considerably. The rest of the work will be up to the gatekeepers. What they leave undone, in turn, will be part of the residual risk of investing—which we can hope will be more rationally priced by the markets than it was just before the scandals.

> *To me, the most important reform in the Sarbanes-Oxley Act of 2002 was actually the budget increase given to the SEC, which allows for the rebuilding of staff resources, expertise, and morale so badly depleted in the preceding decade. This creates at least the possibility of restoring within the agency a professional culture that, among other things, attracts people with a deep commitment to its mission.*

The main focus of the regulatory effort has to be on designing a more effective system of optimal deterrence for corporate managers in a world where both motive and opportunity to cheat remain strong. Increased enforcement resources are one element, as just noted. Optimal penalties are another. The Sarbanes-Oxley Act fixated on criminal enforcement, which is useful only in a limited set of cases of abject corruption. It is less helpful in the more banal but commonplace instances of opportunistic—and heavily rationalized—behavior in the face of ambiguous reporting norms.

The key is a threat of strong sanction to offset the fact that many forms of financial misconduct are not detected or remedied. Some of the civil enforcement reforms of Sarbanes-Oxley are quite helpful here, especially those going to equitable relief measures, such as disgorgement of bonuses and compensation and officer-director bars.[2] The missing piece here may be an adjudicatory system capable of both legal and fact-finding accuracy in the face of complex financial misconduct. A task for the SEC would be the creation of a well-resourced internal administrative proceedings mechanism, with expert judges able to handle these cases capably and expeditiously—an internal equivalent to the Delaware chancery judges. One who looks closely at the cease-and-desist authority granted to the SEC in 1990—noting (a) that in Sarbanes-Oxley, authority was broadened to include officer-director bar power, and (b) that there is a pending legislative proposal to add civil penalty authority as well in administrative proceedings—will see the outlines on which such a system could be built. Administrative proceedings will become the forum in which misbehaving executives are most often tried.

As to disclosure rules, the need for change is relatively low. Even before the scandals, there was an adequate base for enforcing strong transparency requirements. Risk disclosure needs improvement; in particular, the Management's Discussion and Analysis section in companies' periodic reports, which does so much of the heavy lifting with respect to forward-looking disclosure, deserves fundamental rethinking rather than gradual tinkering, especially as we move to a "real-time disclosure" environment. But what many people have said in the aftermath of the scandals is true: everything that was seriously wrong violated existing rules or principles, so that the problem was not that the disclosure regime was filled with large holes.

The lingering question is whether the regulatory system we have is comprehensive enough at the federal level. It does still leave most (if somewhat less) of the responsibility for corporate governance to the states and the exchanges, thus keeping an awkward and mainly uncoordinated separation of powers in place. In theory—and assuming that the right resources and

---

[2] Penalties imposed on the issuer do much less to deter executive misconduct. One reason I am skeptical that private rights of action are as effective a deterrent as they should be is that almost all judgments and settlements in open-market class actions are funded either by the issuer or by its directors' and officers' insurance carrier.

incentives are in place to make the federal bureaucracy an efficient monopolistic regulator—governance of publicly-traded issuers should be centralized. But those are contestable assumptions, and politics makes the exercise an abstraction in any event.

Short of that, however, there will remain something of an "expectations gap" in corporate governance and securities regulation—a promise of more than regulation can actually deliver. There is an open question about whether the sound and fury of Sarbanes-Oxley hurts more than it helps, imposing the costs of uncertainty and disruption on the issuer community (and, ultimately, on the capital markets) while creating mainly only the illusion of real change. Perhaps—but there is a more optimistic view that goes beyond just taking stock of some of the positive changes relating to enforcement and the refurbishing of the professional culture at the SEC. In the end, regulation is always constrained; private actors resolve most of the tensions in corporate governance. In the past decade, actors in the corporate sphere fell into hard-to-break bad habits of excessive deference to (if not celebration of) executive power, so long as reports of good corporate performance kept coming. The uncertainty created by Sarbanes-Oxley and the related regulatory response at least has the virtue of creating cognitive dislocation, providing the occasion for leaders to change habits and renegotiate power without implying that something specific is amiss at the firm. Executives, directors, accountants, lawyers, and securities professionals are all looking around, wondering how to behave in the post-Enron world. Regulators—not just the SEC but also the exchanges, as well as federal and state judges—have a short window of opportunity to exploit the anxious uncertainty and prompt a set of habits that are healthier for investors than the old ones.

The Professionalization of Corporate Directors

MARTIN LIPTON AND JAY W. LORSCH

Unlike the other "professions" on which these papers focus, corporate directors in the United States do not meet the traditional standards to be considered a profession. There is no specific education required and no formal examination that must be passed in order to serve on a corporate board. Other than the fundamental legal standard of conduct encompassed in the business judgment rule, there is no formally adopted or widely accepted code of professional conduct for directors. (At least one of these factors is present in the other professions we have been discussing.) Yet in some other countries (e.g., Australia and the United Kingdom), there have been initiatives to professionalize corporate board members.

Kraakman and Gilson (1991) have argued that a set of professional directors is needed in the U.S.[1] Their definition of "professional" does not require education, exams or standards. Rather, it defines professional directors as persons whose full-time occupation is serving on corporate boards—the implication being that full-time work as a corporate board member makes one a professional. Whether or not one agrees that this definition is adequate, it does highlight another problem with treating directors as professionals. Unlike the other professions, directors—especially independent ones—are almost always part-timers who have, or have had, another full-time career. Given that fact, we want to address two questions: What would be

---

[1] See Reinier Kraakman and Ronald J. Gilson, "Reinventing the Outside Director: An Agenda for Institutional Investors," *Stanford Law Review* 43 (1991): 863.

gained if directors considered themselves, and were considered by society to be, professionals? What would it take to create directors who are truly professionals?

THE CURRENT STATE OF BOARDS

To understand the potential advantages of professionalizing corporate directors, we first need to assess the conduct of boards in the past decade. The news here is both good and bad.

The good news is that most evidence, both anecdotal and from surveys of directors, indicates that during the last decade of the twentieth century, corporate boards became more active and powerful in exercising their responsibilities. Many boards adopted all, or part, of a set of "best practices," such as explicitly approving company strategy and reviewing its effect on corporate performance; evaluating the performance of their CEO; and taking responsibility for assuring management succession.

▶ *Many who had been active in encouraging boardroom reform, including a lot of directors themselves, were shocked by the fact that [the corporate scandals] could take place at a time in which boards seemed to be increasingly diligent and effective. It has become clear that further improvement in the functioning of boards is required.*

Board committees (especially audit, compensation and corporate governance) became more active in their respective domains. A key assumption underlying these practices was that a significant majority of the directors of a company should be independent. These directors were to have their own leader (in addition to the chair/CEO) and were to meet alone periodically. One result of this was that boards were much less beholden to their CEOs in 2000 than they had been in 1990. One concrete piece of evidence of this was, as the decade progressed, the increasing ease and frequency with which boards removed CEOs for poor performance.

In spite of this progress, the bad news was the series of corporate scandals that started with Enron in the fall of 2001 and has continued to the present. Many who had been active in encouraging boardroom reform, including a lot of directors themselves, were shocked by the fact that such scandals could take place at a time in which boards seemed to be increasingly diligent and effective.

Of course, on reflection it is clear that all this malfeasance cannot, and should not, be blamed on boards alone. Audit firms, some consultants, Wall Street banks, and even some law firms and regulatory agencies played a part in shaping these events. Nevertheless, it has become clear that further improvement in the functioning of boards is required.

Calls for such reform have come from the media, Washington, the stock exchanges and the investment community, among others. Many suggestions and ideas have been put forth. At this writing, the two initiatives that are certain to have the greatest consequences are the Sarbanes-Oxley Act of 2002 and the new listing requirements of the stock exchanges. Without going into too much detail, there are two major themes in these laws and regulations. The first is a continuing, but increased, reliance on the critical importance of having independent directors on the board and on key committees. The second is an emphasis on what might be called "design" improvements for boards. The emphasis is not only on who should serve on boards, but also on their leadership structure, on their various committees and their duties (especially those of the audit committee), and on the processes that boards should use to monitor performance, make critical decisions, and offer advice.

While there is a new requirement that each company develop a code of conduct for its management and employees, these two initiatives focus limited attention on the values directors are expected to hold and the goals they are expected to pursue. In essence, the emphasis is on getting directors to do things in an effective manner, rather than explicitly focusing on what they are supposed to achieve. This is not surprising since, historically, the aims of boards have been broad and even somewhat vague. For example, the Delaware corporations statute, and various court decisions there, indicate that directors are responsible for the interests of shareholders *and* the corporation. Within such a broad statement there is a great deal of latitude for boards to choose the ends they are seeking.

Shareholders are a diverse and dynamic population. Some, like hedge funds, are involved in "playing" the market and may be only short-term holders. Others, like public pension funds, use indexing and hold the same stocks year after year. Furthermore, it is not unusual for public companies to see other investors, such as mutual funds, take a large position in their stock for months or years and then disappear almost overnight. One indicator of the dynamic quality of share ownership is that, according to the New York Stock Exchange (NYSE), the mean holding period for shares of its listed companies is now less than a year.[2]

The matter of the goals that boards should seek is further complicated by two other factors. The first is the fact that, in the absence of any compelling legal (or other) standard, directors are free to make their own determinations of the goals they should be seeking. Some believe that their goal should be to build a healthy enterprise for the long term, while others are committed to the proposition that quarter-to-quarter increases in earnings per share (EPS) and share price is the goal. To make all this even more complex, boards rarely, if ever, discuss such goals. It is not an exaggeration to say that directors operate in a vacuum as to the purposes boards ought to be pursuing.

Into this void step the analysts, which is the second complication. Because directors have no clear sense of what shareholders really want, the analysts tell them. They do this by demanding "earnings guidance." Basically, what they want is a goal of EPS improvement for the next quarter and the next. The consequence of this pressure—combined with compensation plans for CEOs and other senior executives that reward the same short-term performance—is a focus on delivering short-term earnings that perpetuates what John Cassidy has labeled "the greed cycle."[3] The strong desire to achieve short-term objectives is a principal reason that managers, as well as boards, have so often used aggressive accounting practices.

[2] See the NYSE Quick Reference Sheet, available at http://www.nyse.com/market-info/p1020656068262.html?displayPage=%2Fmarketinfo%2F1022221393893.html.
[3] See John Cassidy, "The Greed Cycle," *New Yorker,* September 23, 2002, 64.

BENEFITS OF PROFESSIONALIZATION

Given this state of affairs in America's boardrooms, we believe that a case can be made for treating directors in a manner somewhat similar to the way certain other professionals are treated. However, as we shall point out shortly, a major challenge would be how to achieve this objective.

The professionalization of corporate directors would have two benefits. First, it would lead to a clearer understanding of what the goals of boards should be. Just as doctors are charged with assuring patient health and lawyers with acting in the interests of clients, directors could be charged with the responsibility of achieving clear, but broad, objectives. We would argue that for a large public company, the goal of the professional director should be the long-term success of the company. Such a goal would benefit shareholders while also placing emphasis on the company's responsibility to other parties (employees, customers, and suppliers). It would also entail assuring that the company (including its employees) is behaving in a legal and ethical manner. A code of professional conduct for directors should also include an obligation to the investing public to maintain the integrity and transparency of financial reporting.

▶ *The professionalization of corporate directors would lead to a clearer understanding of what the goals of boards should be. We would argue that for a large public company, the goal of the professional director should be the long-term success of the company.*

The second benefit is consistent with the first. Over the past decade, the focus of board improvement has been on what boards are expected to do and how they can best be organized to accomplish their work. We believe that there is every reason to continue this focus. The design of how boards are organized needs to be further improved to deal with the growing complexity of their companies, the increased expectations being placed on boards, and the limits that boards face because of their reliance on outside independent directors who do not have the same knowledge and experience as the officers of the companies.

Professionalizing corporate directors would add a comple-
mentary focus on the purpose of boards. In place of what are
now rather vague objectives, we believe that an explicit professional code for board members would provide clear goals that
boards are meant to achieve. Ideally, this could lead to boards
that not only function effectively, but do so with clear ends in
sight.

CREATING PROFESSIONAL DIRECTORS

Now we come to what may be the toughest question of all.
Assuming professionalizing directors is a great idea, how would
it be accomplished? At first glance it might not seem too difficult. After all, probably fewer than 10,000 people serve on the
boards of publicly listed companies. However, this is quite a
diverse set of people, with different backgrounds (including
CEOs, ex-government officials, investors, and members of various professions, some active, some retired). Furthermore, they
have all had a lot of experience and may hold strong opinions
about their duties as directors. Clearly indoctrinating them into
a common code of conduct is likely to be much more complicated than educating law or medical students—and the latter are
processes that involve years of education and include licensing
exams. It would also be necessary to ensure that professionalization would not increase the exposure of directors to litigation. It
is clear that the imposition of legal liability—whether it be civil
or criminal, and whether it be the pre-Sarbanes-Oxley five years'
potential imprisonment, or the post-Sarbanes-Oxley twenty—
does not eliminate fraud or malpractice by corporate executives,
lawyers, bankers and accountants. To accompany the professionalization of directors with additional legal liability would not
improve their performance; it would simply deter good people
from serving as directors.

A potential starting point for the professionalization process
might be the stock exchanges. For example, if the NYSE were to
endorse a statement of professional conduct (which would not
be significantly more extensive than the corporate guidelines and

ethics codes mandated by the new NYSE rules) that a director of a listed company must promise to uphold when he or she joins its board, it would be a start. While we would not propose an official certifying educational experience or exam, the professional code could be reinforced by educational efforts through the stock exchanges and various educational programs that already exist for new directors. The NYSE rules requiring "indoctrination" for new directors, as well as the director education programs currently being sponsored by the NYSE, are the types of director education we have in mind.

It would be naive to assume that such steps would immediately focus all directors on a clear set of goals, but they would be a start! At least they would be an improvement over the situation in which so many boards find themselves—becoming more efficient and effective, but without clarity as to their goals and purpose.

The proposal by Robert Monks and Allen Sykes[4] to change the law so that corporations would have two sets of directors (the customary management and independent directors nominated by the board, plus three directors specially nominated by institutional shareholders), and the proposed revision of the SEC proxy rules to provide shareholders access to the annual proxy statement to nominate two or three directors, are *not* what we have in mind. While the adoption of such proposals would likely lead to the development of a cadre of "professional" directors, it would also balkanize boards and render them dysfunctional.

Our recommendation is that directors' commitment to professionalism be established and reinforced by means of thorough indoctrination of new directors, annual two- or three-day comprehensive strategic reviews by the board, and directors' attendance at the type of educational programs mentioned above, combined with adherence to the guidelines, charters, and codes mandated by the stock exchanges.

[4] Robert Monks and Allen Sykes, *Capitalism Without Owners Will Fail: A Policymaker's Guide to Reform* (London: Centre for the Study of Financial Innovation, 2002). The full report is available at http://www.ragm.com/library/topics/ragm_sykesPolicyMakersGuide.html.

Comment

Should Directors Be Professionals?

MARGARET M. BLAIR

Martin Lipton and Jay Lorsch have proposed that an important aspect of reform that must happen in the corporate sector is for directors to be more "professional" in the way they go about their job. By this they mean that directors must understand their role as one that is held to very high standards and expectations—not, as has been suggested by other commentators,[1] that they should be people who make their living by being board members, or that they be required to go through "an official certifying educational experience or exam."

On its face, this proposal seems completely unobjectionable, and it is one that I wholeheartedly endorse. The potentially controversial part of their proposal is in what they think the standards and expectations should be. In particular, they argue that "for large public companies, the goal of professional directors should be the long-term success of their company," defined very broadly to include a corporate responsibility to other parties as well as to shareholders. This goal is stated in opposition to a goal of focusing solely on short-term share price performance.

My own academic experience over the past decade suggests that the notion that corporations are creatures of contract whose sole function is maximizing value for shareholders is so entrenched in the business community, in law schools, in MBA programs, in the business press, and in legal practice that advo-

---

[1] See Reinier Kraakman and Ronald J. Gilson, "Reinventing the Outside Director: An Agenda for Institutional Investors," *Stanford Law Review* 43 (1991): 863.

cates of a broader view have had a very difficult time being heard and taken seriously.

It's not so bad for an academic to be an eccentric voice crying in a wilderness full of shareholder primacy advocates. One gets invited to numerous conferences to be the token representative of the quaint idea dismissively referred to as "stakeholder theory."

But Lipton and Lorsch are talking about much more than having a few alternative voices heard at conferences. They are suggesting, for example, that a general professional code should be drawn up for corporate directors that would "provide clear goals that boards are meant to achieve," and that some concerted effort toward director education should be made, perhaps through the stock exchanges. They apparently have in mind that the goal of such director education would be only partly about teaching directors how to be more effective. It would also be about "indoctrinating them in a common code of conduct" that would be based on the broader standard of "long-term success of the company" rather than on short-term share value maximization.

▶ *The notion that corporations are creatures of contract whose sole function is maximizing value for shareholders is so entrenched in the business community, in law schools, in MBA programs, in the business press, and in legal practice that advocates of a broader view have had a very difficult time being heard and taken seriously.*

If this is going to happen, it is going to take a lot more than a few eccentric academic voices arguing that corporate directors have duties to the whole community of interests that make up the corporation. It's going to take a massive shift in the norms that have driven academic scholarship and legal practice for the past two decades.

The relationship between law and norms has been the subject of a small but growing literature in recent years, but little in this literature has addressed how norms come to be established in the first place or how they can be changed if they need to be changed. Questions I would like to know more about, in response to the Lipton and Lorsch proposal, are: How do norms, in general, come into being? How has the particular norm of shareholder primacy come to be so dominant? (It is not just because funds managers have pressured corporate chief financial officers to show consistent quarterly growth in earnings, because the norm has become at least as dominant, if not more so, in academia as it has in board rooms.) And how do norms change, or how can they be changed, once they become established?

Thomas Kuhn taught us decades ago that old paradigms do not die quietly and gracefully.[2] Instead, disciples of the old paradigms argue ever more fiercely in their defense, even as the arguments for the defense get increasingly convoluted and implausible. At some point, however, the debate reaches some kind of tipping point, and the simple elegance of the new paradigm wins out.

I fear that the paradigm of share value maximization is a long way from dying out and that much work will be required to bring Lipton and Lorsch's proposal to pass. Although there are numerous director training programs popping up at law schools, business schools, and consulting firms, these programs generally either start from the shareholder primacy premise or ignore the issue completely and go straight to the nuts and bolts of implementing the Sarbanes-Oxley Act of 2002.

It may turn out that we are closer than I fear to a tipping point, and that changing the paradigm and indoctrinating a new generation of directors in the new paradigm will happen more easily than I think. We have already seen that Michael Jensen—one of the late twentieth century's leading advocates of shareholder primacy and of hostile takeovers as a mechanism for enforcing it—has now conceded that a myopic focus on short-term share value can be harmful and that the appropriate goal of officers and directors must be what he calls "enlightened value maximization."[3] He has also conceded that "an overvalued stock

[2] Thomas S. Kuhn, *The Structure of Scientific Revolutions* (Chicago: University of Chicago Press, 1962).
[3] Michael C. Jensen, "Value Maximization, Stakeholder Theory, and the Corporate Objective Function," *Journal of Applied Corporate Finance* 14 (2001): 8.

can be as damaging to the long-run health of a company as an undervalued stock."[4] Other shareholder primacy advocates, who argued in the 1980s that corporate directors should be required to be passive in the face of a hostile takeover that offered shareholders an immediate premium over the prior trading price of the stock, are now retreating to a view that the goal of directors should be to maximize share value in the long run.

Moreover, it is instructive to note what Michael Jensen says directors and officers must do to maximize long-run financial value: "In order to maximize value, corporate managers must not only satisfy, but enlist the support of, all corporate stakeholders—customers, employees, managers, suppliers, local communities. Top management plays a critical role in this function through its leadership and effectiveness in creating, projecting, and sustaining the company's strategic vision."[5] Enlightened value maximization, he goes on, "uses much of the structure of stakeholder theory but accepts maximization of the long-run value of the firm as the criterion for making the requisite trade-offs among its stakeholders."[6]

Thus, it turns out that as shareholder primacy advocates have become "enlightened," they have discovered that value creation involves vision, risk taking, and complex trade-offs among a variety of participants in the business enterprise of the firm. The implicit prescriptions for director behavior are, unsurprisingly, rather vague—but they sound a lot like the prescriptions that come out of what Lynn Stout and I call a "team production" model of corporate law. We argue that the role of corporate directors is to mediate among members of the corporate team, making decisions in the interest of the corporate entity, which serves as a proxy for the combined interests of all the team members. Actually, in practice, the goal of making decisions in the interest of the corporate entity may be indistinguishable from the goal of maximizing long-term shareholder value. Neither

4 Joseph Fuller and Michael C. Jensen, "Just Say No to Wall Street" (Working Paper no. 02-01, Amos Tuck School of Business at Dartmouth College, Hanover, NH, February 2001).
5 Jensen, "Value Maximization," 9.
6 Jensen, "Value Maximization," 9.

goal provides courts with a way to tell whether directors are doing their job in an optimal way.

So if we cannot distinguish in practice among the goals of long term share value maximization on the one hand, and overall wealth creation and long-term success of the enterprise on the other, why should it matter what metaphor or language we use to describe the duties of directors? The reason is that language influences behavior because it is an expression of the norm. The language of share value maximization is a language of zero-sum games, of in-groups and out-groups, in which one group within the organization is seen as primary and the others, necessarily, as secondary. There is powerful evidence from so-called social dilemma games that such language alone tends to undermine the natural tendencies that people seem to have to engage in cooperative behavior.

▶ *We argue that the role of corporate directors is to mediate among members of the corporate team, making decisions in the interest of the corporate entity, which serves as a proxy for the combined interests of all the team members.*

By contrast, the language of team production, and of overall wealth creation by and for the team, is language that suggests to corporate participants that they are all part of the same in-group, and that there may be win-win solutions if they all cooperate.

Of course, the language of team production can also be used to cover up bad decisions and reduce accountability. It solves no problems by itself. But if directors are to be better educated and trained in order to try to elicit more successful performance, it seems clear to me that directors who start from the premise that their job is to oversee the work of a team, and to mediate among team members to encourage them to work together to achieve value-creating corporate goals, are more likely to consider each decision in terms of its impact on each of the relevant and important stakeholders, as well as on the overall goals of the corporation. And in the long run, making decisions this way seems more likely to produce sustainable long-run value creation than allowing decision making to be driven by what directors and officers think analysts want to hear at the next analysts' meeting.

Professionalization Does Not Mean Power or Accountability

DAMON SILVERS

Corporate boards are dominated by corporate officers and are therefore not an effective check on those officers when they act to harm the company, its shareholders, or the public. There is an obvious answer to this problem: create genuine accountability for board members outside the closed circle of the board and the CEO. But this answer is almost literally unspeakable for too many commentators on this subject, who tie themselves up in knots trying to figure out how to solve the problem of the board without really diminishing the power of the CEO or introducing any countervailing power into the board room. This is like trying to solve the problem of slavery without actually freeing the slaves. You can spend all day exhorting them to be free—you can call them independent, or even professionals, and demand that they run free—but at the end of the day, there they are, still in chains.

In contrast, worker pension funds and other institutional investors are looking to make long-term investors a real counterbalance to management power in the board room. On May 15, 2003, the AFL-CIO filed a rulemaking petition with the Securities and Exchange Commission, asking the Commission to democratize the director election process.[1] The petition asks

[1] The petition can be found at the AFL-CIO website, http://www.aflcio.org.

the Commission to adopt rules giving long-term significant investors in public companies the right to have short slates of directors they nominate listed on management's proxy, along with management board candidates. This proposal for access to the proxy is designed to give long-term institutional investors voice, not to facilitate takeovers. We suspect that access to the proxy, while rarely used—by its very availability as an option—will make dialogue between boards and investors much more substantive.[2]

The "shareholder access" proposal is a response to the peculiar catch-22 quality of corporate boards. Institutional investors have sought for years to directly rein in the power of CEOs. First they tried shareholder proposals, only to be told that those proposals can address only a very limited range of subject matter and are precatory—meaning that boards can ignore majority votes. So shareholders then tried binding shareholder proposals, only to be told that as a general matter, such proposals are an impermissible intrusion on the power of the board. In frustration, shareholders turned to litigation (e.g., bringing derivative actions to address scandalous executive pay practices), only to be told that this is an area where boards are sovereign—and that if shareholders have a problem with the way their company is being managed, they should change the board.

▶ *For long-term investors like worker pension funds, the apparent choices are to acquiesce to managerial misconduct, sell the stock, or support a corporate takeover. These are not acceptable choices for worker pension funds with long-term investment objectives and indexed holdings that cover the whole market.*

Here's where the catch-22 happens: If shareholders try to change the board, they will find that the incumbents control access to both the company proxy and the company treasury, and that insurgents have to mount their candidacy at their own

[2] Editors' note: As of September 2004, the prospects for the "shareholder access" initiative remain uncertain. The SEC staff has circulated, for public comment, a proposed new rule that would give shareholders the power, in specified circumstances, to directly nominate candidates for a minority of board seats. However, the SEC's commissioners have yet to vote on this or any alternative proposal.

expense—an expense that, for large capitalization companies, is likely to be in the millions of dollars. Actually, boards tend to be changed only in the course of takeover battles—battles that rarely occur in large capitalization companies and that are fraught with dangers of their own, from the perspective of long-term institutional investors.

For long-term investors like worker pension funds, the apparent choices are to acquiesce to managerial misconduct, sell the stock, or support a corporate takeover. These are not acceptable choices for worker pension funds with long-term investment objectives and indexed holdings that cover the whole market. As noted in a recent report by the Conference Board's Commission on Public Trust and Private Enterprise, such "stock owners" have interests that are more closely aligned with the corporate law duties of directors, to act in the long-term interests of the corporation and its shareholders, than do more short-term-focused hedge funds or arbitrageurs.[3] That is why organizations like the Council of Institutional Investors and large pension funds like CALPERS are supporting the idea of democratizing the board election process. It is the only responsible choice that funds have.

Martin Lipton and Jay Lorsch nonetheless oppose the idea of democratizing the board process. They suggest professionalizing corporate directors as a strategy for improving board performance. On the surface, this is an appealing idea, but there is a real irony to the idea of professionalization as a response to the recent corporate crisis.

The modern professions—medicine, law, accounting, and engineering—were consciously set up to insulate their members from market pressures on the quality and price of their work product. But the power of professionalism as a counterweight to market forces appears to have reached its heyday in the postwar years and to have declined significantly in recent years, as boundaries between professions and professional codes of conduct have weakened.

[3] Conference Board, "Commission on Public Trust and Private Enterprise: Findings and Recommendations" (New York: Conference Board, 2002).

In particular, the role of the accounting and legal profession in recent corporate scandals can be seen as a window into the inability of previously effective professional cultures to restrain auditors, attorneys, and others from doing anything that might be profitable to them in the short term. It thus seems fair to ask: If the far stronger professions of law and public accounting couldn't restrain those professionals from contributing to the recent wave of corporate misconduct, how are embryonic standards for boards of directors to have any chance of changing board behavior in the face of the CEO's much more direct power over directors?

▶ *If the far stronger professions of law and public accounting couldn't restrain those professionals from contributing to the recent wave of corporate misconduct, how are embryonic standards for boards of directors to have any chance of changing board behavior in the face of the CEO's much more direct power over directors?*

Greater training and education for directors might help address the sort of problem illustrated in a recent example. At the time of the collapse of Enron, one of its directors was an employee of Alliance Capital—a large money management firm that had been accumulating Enron stock on behalf of its clients. In response to questions from the press, a senior officer of Alliance described the board position held by an Alliance officer as a "personal perk." To the extent that this view of serving on a public company board is still prevalent, it would seem that education and training are needed.

Codes of conduct could also help directors do their jobs—but only if the codes are crafted to really push directors toward actually exercising oversight. For example, many directors believe that it is inappropriate for them to have direct contact with shareholders. A code of conduct that reinforced that misperception would be harmful, whereas one that made clear that directors have an obligation to communicate with shareholders would be making a meaningful step toward improving board performance.

Obviously, there is likely to be significant resistance to democratizing the board from some sectors of the corporate community. But before resisting this concept, management should consider what alternative model of accountability it would prefer. The truth is that too many CEOs appear to prefer no accountability at all—but after the scandals of the past two years, that is not an option. The alternatives—government regulation in the model of the Sarbanes-Oxley Act of 2002 or the corporate control market—appear, if anything, to be less appetizing to CEOs than a genuinely democratized corporate governance process.

The Limits of Corporate Law in Promoting Good Corporate Governance

MICHAEL KLAUSNER

Discussions of corporate governance reform often combine pre-scriptions for legal reform with prescriptions for better gover-nance practices. Both sets of prescriptions—for better law and for better practices—typically focus on the board of directors, and particularly outside or "independent" directors. The assump-tion is that the law can affect the governance behavior of the board by establishing roles for outside directors and by motivat-ing independent directors to do a good job. The extent to which law can promote good governance in the boardroom, however, is quite limited. To a large extent, good corporate governance must come from other sources of motivation, especially to the extent that a source of good governance is the independent director. This comment will briefly outline the limits of corpo-rate law in promoting good corporate governance and in doing so help clarify the gap that must be filled by nonlegal influences, including the sort of norms that Martin Lipton and Jay Lorsch emphasize.

TRADITIONAL CORPORATE LAW

Traditionally, there have been three sets of legal rules designed to induce directors to govern in the interest of shareholders. First, there are fiduciary duties and procedural rules that provide lawyers with incentives to bring suits to enforce those duties. Second, there are shareholder voting rules, which allow shareholders to replace directors whom they view as having failed to act in their interests. Third, there are disclosure rules that require management to disseminate information regarding a company's finances and operations. One might also add as a fourth set of rules those rules governing hostile acquisitions, which allow shareholders to separate themselves from inadequate management by selling all their shares to an acquiror. These bodies of law, however, impose a fairly minimal inducement to directors, particularly to independent directors, to govern well. They can be severe in cases of self-dealing by corrupt management, but they are actually weak—and necessarily so—when it comes to promoting affirmatively good governance practices in the boardroom.

▶ *Notwithstanding reports in the press about the legal risks directors face, their risk of out-of-pocket damage payments is negligible. We have found virtually no case in which an outside director has actually paid money out of his or her own pocket, despite the fact that every year dozens of suits are brought under corporate or securities laws naming them as defendants.*

In contrast to many other areas of activity, the fiduciary duties applicable to outside directors do not, as a practical matter, pose a realistic threat of out-of-pocket liability unless a director has engaged in theft or blatant self-dealing. In other areas, one can expect to pay damages if one fails to meet a certain standard of competence and care. Negligence standards apply, for example, to doctors, automobile drivers, engineers and others. Although these people have other motivations to do a good job, the threat of liability, at least for some, provides an additional motivation. Notwithstanding reports in the press about the legal risks directors face, their risk of out-of-pocket damage payments is negligible. In ongoing research with Bernard Black and Brian Cheffins, we have found virtually no case in which an outside director has actually paid money out of his or her own pocket, despite the fact that every year dozens of suits are brought under corporate or securities laws naming them as defendants, and hundreds of suits are filed against their companies.[1]

[1] See Bernard S. Black, Brian R. Cheffins, and Michael Klausner, "Outside Director

In many cases, suits fail at the outset because the rules governing the pleading of shareholder suits impose a significant bar to plaintiffs regarding what they must credibly allege regarding outside directors' misdeeds. Others are dismissed later under the "business judgment rule," a judicial doctrine under which courts decline to second-guess a board's business decision so long as the decision was informed and so long as there was no conflict of interest involved. Cases that are not dismissed almost always settle on terms that have the corporation and the corporation's directors' and officers' (D&O) liability insurer make a payment to the shareholders. There is nothing nefarious going on in these settlements. What happens is a logical consequence of the rules governing shareholder suits, a corporation's power to indemnify its directors, D&O insurance, and most importantly, the incentives of all sides to settle shareholder suits without reaching inside the defendants' own pockets.

We have found that this pattern of de facto immunity to out-of-pocket liability exists not just in the U.S., but also in Australia, Britain, Canada, France, Germany, and Japan—countries that span both common and civil law traditions. We suspect that the pattern is universal. Moreover, looking back at the history of legal rules governing the liability of corporate directors, one finds that when this pattern is disturbed, and outside directors are threatened with liability, either the market or lawmakers step in to reinstate directors' protection.[2]

Shareholder voting has a similarly weak impact on directors' incentives to do a good job. Under the law, shareholders have the power to replace a board of directors, but they virtually never even try to do so outside the context of a hostile acquisition, which I discuss below. The reason for their passivity is the classic

Liability," available online at http://ssrn.com/abstract=382422; Bernard Black, Brian Cheffins, and Michael Klausner, "Liability Risk for Outside Directors: A Cross-Border Analysis," *European Financial Management* 11 (forthcoming 2005), available online at http://ssrn.com/abstract=557070.

[2] See Bernard Black, Brian Cheffins, and Michael Klausner, "Liability Risk for Outside Directors: A Cross-Border Analysis," *European Financial Management* 11 (forthcoming 2005), available online at http://ssrn.com/abstract=557070; Bernard S. Black and Brian R. Cheffins, "Outside Director Liability Across Countries," available online at http://ssrn.com/abstract=438321.

collective action problem that shareholders face. A shareholder who mounts such a campaign must pay the cost of doing so up front. The shareholder's gain, if it materializes, will take the form of a better managed company and higher share value. Unless that shareholder holds a large block of shares, his personal cost-benefit analysis of a campaign to replace the board will not support mounting the campaign. Moreover, even for a large shareholder, unless a substantial proportion of a company's other shares are also held by one or more block holders, it will be difficult to get the attention of enough other shareholders, let alone induce them to spend time analyzing whether the insurgent slate of directors will create value that the incumbents have not.

The third area of law that may be of some help to shareholders is the securities laws. These laws require a company to disclose, on a periodic basis and prior to issuing securities, all material information regarding its finances and operations. These laws work very well in day-to-day settings. Companies regularly disclose material information to the market and market prices generally respond with amazing speed. The disclosure process is managed by company executives. Difficulties occasionally arise, however, when a company is having financial or operational trouble, and management cuts corners in its disclosures. It is exceedingly difficult for outside board members to discover that this is going on. As a matter of the law on the books, they are potentially liable for failure to disclose material information, but they are rightfully accorded defenses if they have exercised a reasonable degree of oversight. Consequently, suits brought under the securities laws against outside directors are commonly dismissed. Moreover, even for suits that are not dismissed early on, the rules governing indemnification and D&O insurance, and the incentives of all parties to settle, render the threat of out-of-pocket liability essentially illusory for an outside director. Thus, once again, the threat of sanction has little direct effect on governance behavior in the boardroom.

The law of hostile takeovers may be somewhat more helpful, but not by much. Theoretically, if management of a company fails to maximize the value of the business, someone else will be interested in stepping in to do so. If management is not willing to turn over the reins, a prospective acquiror can instead approach the shareholders directly by making a "tender offer" to buy their shares at a premium. Under law developed during the 1980s, however, a board is permitted to obstruct this transaction by adopting a "poison pill," a dilutive mechanism that will stop the acquiror in its tracks until the target board of directors removes it. The law governing a target board's decision whether to remove a poison pill and allow a takeover to proceed is oddly schizophrenic. It allows the board to keep the pill in place in the face of a premium bid, if the board believes the bid is for some reason inadequate. ("Grossly inadequate" is the preferred term of targets, their bankers and their lawyers, for whom no bid is ever merely "inadequate.") The law even allows a board to sell the company to a party offering a lower bid—but only if the competing bid would provide target shareholders with stock in the combined company. Thankfully, the law does not allow a board to sell the company for cash if a higher cash bid is available. Once the board decides to sell the company for cash, it must sell to the highest bidder.

Fortunately for shareholders, there is an end-run around a board that uses its legal power to resist an attractive takeover offer. Shareholders can vote out an incumbent board and replace it with a board that will disable the pill and allow the acquisition to proceed. Experience has shown that the immediate prospect of a premium bid is enough to get shareholders to overcome their collective action problem and vote their shares in this context.

The threat that an acquiror will appear in the future, and that shareholders will replace their board in order to sell their company, may provide some incentive for a board to govern well. Hostile takeovers, however, typically occur at price premiums of thirty percent or more over market. This suggests that management must be doing a very bad job—running a company at less than 70 percent of potential—for an acquiror to step in and rescue shareholders. So perhaps the threat of a hostile takeover creates an incentive for a board not to govern horribly, but it does not create an incentive for the board to govern well.

In sum, it is difficult to imagine that these sets of legal rules have a significant direct effect on the incentives of a board of directors to govern in an affirmatively effective manner. To the extent boards are attentive and diligent in their oversight of management, it is not (or at least should not be) out of a fear of out-of-pocket liability, or a fear of being voted out of office, or a fear of having their company acquired. Their motivation must lie elsewhere.

Moreover, if the law were changed to increase the likelihood that outside directors would be penalized more severely for inadequate governance, corporate governance could well suffer. Many people would decline to serve as directors, particularly those with substantial assets or reputations at stake, and others would become excessively defensive in their oversight role. In addition, directors' fees would have to increase to compensate for the heightened personal risk borne by those who do serve. Paradoxically, this could have the effect of compromising the independence of directors for whom fees become a meaningful portion of total income. Directors in this position might hesitate to rock the boat, let alone resign, in the face of management decisions that they find troubling.

▶ *If the law were changed to increase the likelihood that outside directors would be penalized more severely for inadequate governance, corporate governance could well suffer. Many people would decline to serve as directors, particularly those with substantial assets or reputations at stake, and others would become excessively defensive in their oversight role.*

SARBANES-OXLEY AND RELATED REFORM EFFORTS

The Sarbanes-Oxley Act of 2002 and the related changes in New York Stock Exchange and NASDAQ rules, all following in the wake of the Enron and other corporate scandals, imposed a set of structure and process rules on boards. For example, a majority of directors must be "independent," a term the rules define in great detail; audit, compensation, and nominating/governance committees must be constituted with all independent directors; and independent directors must meet alone periodically, with one among them identified publicly as the director presiding over those meetings.

Leaving aside whether these legal rules, on balance, promote good governance more than other structures and procedures that boards might instead adopt on their own, it is reasonable to expect that structure and process, in general, will have an impact on directors' governance behavior, and that many of the recent reforms may have a positive impact on the governance of many companies. The nature of the impact, however, is to place directors in settings in which other motivations will ideally take effect and lead them to govern effectively. For example, an independent director, sitting in a compensation committee meeting, will not challenge a management recommendation or recommend firing a CEO solely because management is not present at the meeting. Nor will independent directors meeting out of management's presence necessarily put in the hard work needed to understand a difficult issue that they fear the CEO is minimizing, solely because the CEO is not present at the meeting. A director will not become diligent as a result of structure or process alone. There must be further inducements, whether they be carrots or sticks, and the recent reforms do not alter the stick of liability risk, nor do they provide any carrots.

IF NOT LAW, WHAT CAN PROMOTE GOOD GOVERNANCE?

A full discussion of the extra-legal forces that can motivate good governance in the boardroom lies beyond the scope of this brief essay. One obvious source of extra-legal influence is economic. If board members hold substantial blocks of a company's shares throughout their tenure on the board, they would presumably be more attentive in the boardroom. It would be impractical for the law to impose such a requirement, since the number of shares that constitute a block substantial enough to motivate good governance depends on how wealthy a particular board member is. Nonetheless, boards could adopt this policy on their own and disclose the policy, the directors' shareholdings, and at least some additional details in their filings with the Securities and Exchange Commission. Shareholder advocates have been pressing for this arrangement for some time.

Professional norms are another potential force motivating good governance, presumably a force that already explains in part why governance fiascos, prominent as they have been, have actually been rare. These norms are fostered by the financial press every time they write a story that exposes bad board behavior, and, on occasion, when they write a story applauding good board behavior. Shareholder suits that shine a light on bad behavior, and that at times generate court decisions, help create and disseminate norms as well—even if they do ultimately settle at no out-of-pocket cost to the directors.[3] Codes of best practices written by management and shareholder associations, while often bland in the extreme and resembling lessons one learned in kindergarten, have an impact as well. Lipton and Lorsch's prescription of more deliberate norm creation and dissemination and director education is certainly worth a try as well.

In conclusion, while the law can deter egregious self-serving behavior, it can only go so far in promoting good governance in the boardroom. The slack must be picked up by economic and social forces. Those forces already exist, but perhaps they can be enhanced as Lipton and Lorsch suggest.

[3] Edward Rock, "Saints and Sinners: How Does Delaware Corporate Law Work?," *U.C.L.A. Law Review* 44 (1997): 1009.

Chapter 6

The Auditor as Gatekeeper: A Perilous Expectations Gap

WILLIAM R. KINNEY, JR.

My assignment is to address three related questions about the independent auditor as a gatekeeper for corporate responsibility: What are the auditing profession's obligations to the public interest vis-à-vis corporate misconduct? How well have auditors performed, over the past decade, in restraining corporate misconduct? And what steps should be taken to improve the auditing profession's performance in restraining corporate misconduct? This difficult assignment is further complicated by presumptions implicit in the questions, as well as by the public's emerging expectations in a rapidly changing environment.

THE AUDITING PROFESSION'S OBLIGATIONS AND REASONABLE EXPECTATIONS

For the past century, American corporations have hired independent auditors to add credibility to financial statements that corporate managers prepare. Each corporation hires the auditor it wishes, and a competent independent auditor's report reduces financial misstatement risk for investors. Lower financial misstatement risk can increase a corporation's stock price, thus

The author acknowledges the helpful comments and suggestions of Carolyn Kinney, Robert Libby, Zoe-Vonna Palmrose, and Neil Schreiber on earlier drafts of this paper.

reducing its cost of capital, and can also reduce the costs of production and distribution for its goods and services through better contract terms with workers, suppliers, and customers.

To increase the stock price, financial statements must be prepared using methods that investors find relevant for their decisions, such as generally accepted accounting principles (GAAP). Because managers have an interest in financial statements other than their quality, a competent independent auditor is needed to assure investors that GAAP has been carefully applied and results properly displayed. The auditor must have an unquestioned reputation for integrity, because the auditor may need to correct assertions of the corporation that hired the auditor.

The application of GAAP requires many assumptions about a business, its plans, and its prospects, and therefore requires the managers of that business to make many judgments and measurement choices. By analogy, one might imagine Olympic figure skaters, each charged with scoring his or her own performance according to Olympic scoring criteria. Choices made by one skater would affect the evaluation of that skater and of other skaters, as well as the welfare of outsiders. In such a system, we would expect each skater's self-score to be higher than a score prepared by an independent expert judge. Furthermore, a reputable expert judge hired by the skater to assess whether the skater's own scoring is reasonable or fair, given Olympic scoring criteria, would probably lower the skater's self-score only enough to bring it within the upper limit of a "reasonable" or "fair" range.

Our financial reporting system works remarkably like the hypothetical skating example. The principal has a lot of power and discretion, and there is pressure on the hired "referee" to allow some principal-serving bias in the principal's self-scoring process. Also, the application of both Olympic skating performance criteria and GAAP is somewhat subjective, and insiders' and outsiders' welfare depends on the resulting scores in both contexts. Of course, real-world skaters do not get to keep their own score and hire their own confirming experts—but corporations do.

Under a traditional view of the auditor's responsibilities, based on generally accepted auditing standards (GAAS), a corporation hires an auditor to limit financial misstatement risk by certifying that its managers' financial statements comply with GAAP and are fairly presented in all material respects. This means limiting the risk of sizable (i.e., material) accidental bookkeeping errors and intentional financial statement fraud. The auditor's responsibilities for financial misstatement risk include noting extreme corporate business risk through warnings of impending corporate doom via a "going concern" paragraph. The auditor must also limit some types of corporate misconduct risk by searching for possible financial statement fraud on the part of management and for extreme self-serving biases in the corporation's accounting choices, and by disclosing known material illegal acts by the corporation. Thus, traditionally, financial misstatement risk has included some, but not all, corporate misconduct risk and corporate business risk, and independent auditors have had some responsibility for limiting these included portions.

▶ *These recent criticisms imply an expanded view of the auditor's responsibilities—and indicate that an auditor hired by a corporation is expected to investigate, and to limit to an acceptable level, all aspects of corporate business risk and corporate misconduct risk, as well as the traditional financial misstatement risk. As a practical matter, how is a competent independent auditor, trained in accounting and financial statement auditing, to survive with these expanded responsibilities?*

In recent years, auditors have been criticized for allowing excessive corporate misconduct risk by not correcting small biases in managers' accounting choices and by accepting (or facilitating) managers' designs of transactions specifically to achieve a desired financial statement treatment within GAAP. They have also been criticized for not reporting managers' excessive consumption of perquisites of office. In addition, they have been criticized for failing to warn investors about corporate business risk due to possible declines in business prospects that fall short of business failure, as well as for failing to warn investors about poor decisions by management, risky management decisions, and lax internal controls.

These recent criticisms imply an expanded view of the auditor's responsibilities—and indicate that an auditor hired by a corporation is expected to investigate, and to limit to an acceptable level, all aspects of corporate business risk and corporate misconduct risk, as well as the traditional financial misstatement risk. It is as if the auditor is to be a public watchdog or a corporate responsibility gatekeeper for regulators, corporate governance officials, stockholders, and the general public, in order to protect them from foolhardy, careless, imprudent, or unscrupulous corporate executives and other perils of the marketplace. These expanded expectations entail more than limiting financial misstatement risk with respect to GAAP criteria.

How can the auditor meet these expanded responsibilities? What are objective criteria (comparable to criteria for scoring a triple axel in Olympic figure skating) for reliably measuring business risks, measuring inefficiencies, and determining when reportable misconduct exists? And what substantive expertise is needed to investigate and apply such criteria in practice?

As a practical matter, how is a competent independent auditor, trained in accounting and financial statement auditing, to survive with these expanded responsibilities? An auditor who must compete with other auditors for a corporation's favor to win audit contracts faces production cost pressures that limit possible investigation efforts. When an auditor discovers and publicly reports problems, the corporation may fire the audit firm on the spot, in which case the firm loses all future income from the corporation. Furthermore, such an auditor is often sued for not discovering and reporting the problems sooner. Ask yourself this: Is it reasonable to expect the Big Four auditing partnerships—private businesses that together comprise about four thousand partners whose total audit fees are less than $10 billion per year— effectively to limit all aspects of financial misstatement risk, corporate business risk, and corporate misconduct risk for a $10 trillion economy?

THE AUDITOR'S PERFORMANCE IN CONSTRAINING CORPORATE MISCONDUCT

The past decade has been a remarkable period of unparalleled economic growth, social and technological change, and highly visible corporate misconduct. The economic growth was accompanied by information technology developments and regulatory changes that facilitated securities trading, and it drew many new individual investors with heightened interest in "earnings surprise"—that is, whether reported earnings met or exceeded analysts' forecasts. Stock options were increasingly popular for managers' compensation—in part, some say, because of "loose" accounting for options under GAAP. Options provided incentives for managers to manipulate reported earnings, even by small amounts, in order to manage earnings surprise and increase their options' value.

A rapidly changing environment increased the relative importance of accounting estimates and new types of transactions whose results cannot be readily measured using traditional GAAP. Attempts by accounting standards setters to tighten GAAP to provide a "bright line" for measurement became the basis for managers' structuring transactions to "just miss" financial statement recognition, with auditors sometimes hired to advise how best to do it. Thus, at a time when motivation for biased, "self-scoring" judgments by managers increased, more transactions with accounting "wiggle room" increased the opportunity for earnings manipulation by managers. Furthermore, in assuming that their competitors had manipulated reported earnings, some managers may have rationalized misrepresentation as necessary to maintaining their own corporation's competitive position.

How well has the auditing profession performed in the past decade? Unfortunately, the profession's increasing concern with client confidentiality has limited independent research to document its possible successes, thus hiding the value of its services. We cannot observe the profession's success at (a) correcting accounting errors and financial statement fraud before financial statements are issued (although prior research clearly shows that auditors do that), (b) helping managers make better initial accounting measurement choices, (c) independently warning managers of potential going concern problems before a going concern paragraph becomes necessary, or (d) facilitating improved internal controls through auditors' letters to managers and audit committees. We also have no measure of the reduction of the cost of capital or the benefits of better resource allocation made possible by our system of audited financial reporting. Thus, we have no individual audit firm's data on, or profession-wide measure of, the probably sizable benefits of auditing.

On the other hand, a growing body of data is available for studying auditors' alleged performance failures. Some managers have structured transactions to comply with GAAP but to impair fair presentation, and their auditors have continued to certify GAAP compliance. In other cases, auditors have not discovered material misstatements; GAAS may have been inadequate for discovery, or the auditors may not have followed GAAS. There have also been cases in which auditors appear to have discovered extreme corporate misconduct, or seemingly should have known about impending corporate doom, but did not properly report the problem.

▶ *At a time when motivation for biased, "self-scoring" judgments by managers increased, more transactions with accounting "wiggle room" increased the opportunity for earnings manipulation by managers. Furthermore, in assuming that their competitors had manipulated reported earnings, some managers may have rationalized misrepresentation as necessary to maintaining their own corporation's competitive position.*

What overall conclusions can we draw about performance? First, if the auditor's responsibility for financial misstatement risk is measured by technical compliance with GAAP, then performance is relatively good. However, if the auditor's main function is to be a corporate watchdog, or a gatekeeper for corporate misconduct who guards against all corporate business risk and corporate misconduct risk, then the auditor's performance falls far short of the public's expanding expectations.

IMPROVING THE AUDITOR'S PERFORMANCE IN RESTRAINING CORPORATE MISCONDUCT

In the short term, and within the traditional framework, we can improve GAAP and GAAS, and we can facilitate improved independence, objectivity, and perceived integrity among auditors. As to GAAP, the Financial Accounting Standards Board (FASB) and the Securities and Exchange Commission are exploring principles-based accounting standards that may focus managers and auditors on judgments about fair presentation of financial results rather than a bright line that can be exploited by transactions structuring. In my view, the Sarbanes-Oxley Act of 2002 enhances the FASB's performance potential by uncoupling standards-setting from corporate executives' direct financial influence (indirect influence remains to the extent that Congress continues micromanaging accounting standards setting). Sarbanes-Oxley also properly focuses managers' attention on their responsibility for "fair presentation" beyond mere technical GAAP compliance and provides visible penalties for violations.

For the longer term, if society wants auditors to report on an expanded framework based on corporate business risk and corporate misconduct risk beyond GAAP and fair presentation, then we must first develop objective criteria for measuring business risk and misconduct risk. If such criteria can be developed, their implementation will be costly and will impede managers' pursuit of innovative and potentially profitable but risky strategies. The Sarbanes-Oxley Act's mandates regarding internal quality controls for management self-assessment and for auditor reporting offer hope for some progress, but measurement criteria are limited to financial controls.

As to GAAS, standards for auditing practice can be improved through better methods of evaluating corporate internal control processes and better analytical procedures that exploit information technology in monitoring information systems, monitoring business processes, and assessing financial misstatement risk. If society wants auditors to limit all corporate business risk and corporate misconduct risk, then auditors must be trained to detect excessive risk-taking and corporate misconduct. They must learn more about strategy and forecasting, as well as criminology and law across more than the securities acts. Further, our system of audited financial reporting presumes a degree of trust and trustworthiness among participants. Auditors' second-guessing of all-important business decisions and searching for managers' possible criminal and exploitive behavior would make for a much different environment.

As to auditors' integrity and objectivity and perceptions of their independence, the primary tool of Congress and regulators has been the ban on audit firms' providing nonaudit services to their audit clients. But banning all nonaudit services would still leave uncovered serious problems, such as lax audit firm monitoring of audit engagement partners in the field. Service bans also raise the cost to corporate managers of getting advice, and may raise the cost and lower the quality of auditing. Service bans and the SEC's new one-year "cooling off" period for audit personnel hired by an audit client will reduce the pool of talented individuals wanting to be auditors.

For the longer term, we may need to reconsider the legal structure of auditing, encompassing the nature of private audit contracts, auditor compensation, auditor legal responsibilities, and the parameters of litigation. Private contracting for audits is efficient and not necessarily in conflict with the public's expectations. Also, the Sarbanes-Oxley Act's focus on the independent audit committee (rather than on corporate managers) as the auditor's "client" may be helpful, as may the SEC's new rules restricting audit partner compensation for nonaudit services.

Problems will remain, however, if the auditor who has been hired by a corporation's audit committee and who discovers and reports bad results still loses his or her income stream and faces potentially ruinous lawsuits. It seems essential to establish some mechanism for compensating auditors who act in the public's interest, as well as a more efficient system for private lawsuits. Also, to continue the substantial economic advantages of private audit contracts, regulators must somehow allow auditors reasonable freedom to be both efficient and effective in their audits.

If we as a society are serious about expecting auditors to detect and report poor or risky corporate performance and corporate misconduct, then adequate incentives for them to do so must be in place. This may require different audit contracting, litigation, and regulatory structures. Otherwise, good auditors will shun bad clients, and bad clients will deceive low-quality auditors. Surely, this is not in the public's interest.

Comment

The Audit and the Auditor's Central Role

JOHN H. BIGGS

There is a dangerous gap between what the investing public expects in an audit of a public company and what the auditing profession considers feasible to deliver. Professor Kinney's paper provides an excellent analytic framework for examining the nature of this gap in terms of three fundamental categories of risk: financial misstatement risk, corporate business risk, and corporate misconduct risk.

I wonder, though, about Professor Kinney's motivating statement that "American corporations have hired independent auditors to add credibility to financial statements that corporate managers prepare." Considering the strict statutory and regulatory requirements of the Securities and Exchange Commission that have been passed since the 1930s, the stock exchange listing requirements, and the whole panoply of audit committee powers, duties, and expectations, how can we expect corporate officers to believe they are exercising management judgment in engaging an independent auditor to "add credibility to [their] financial statements"?

I suspect that most simply believe that they must do so in order to stay in business, and treat the relationship with an elaborated protocol (still further elaborated by the Sarbanes-Oxley Act of 2002 and the New York Stock Exchange's new listing requirements). The hiring of an independent auditor seems more a compliance decision than a management decision—in fact, under Sarbanes–Oxley, management is not even allowed to make the decision.

It is interesting to speculate about what companies would do if the relationship with the audit attest function were totally voluntary. Surely the market-driven need for credibility would be significant. However, many firms might choose to forego the expense and hassle of the audit if they had a sufficient reputation for integrity (e.g., Warren Buffett might decide he would save the shareholders the millions he must spend for corporate audits of his empire.) Also, many highly regulated companies might rely on the examinations conducted by their regulators. This was not uncommon for financial service companies in the prerequirement era of the early decades of the twentieth century.

It would be interesting to know the prevalence of audits for private companies. One might surmise that the demand for an audit would rise for such companies as the number of outside investors, especially institutional ones, increases. But wouldn't family-owned enterprises opt to save the substantial costs of a full outside audit and hire outside accounting professionals in a more purposeful way?

There is a powerful motive to hire major accounting firms as auditors to gain access to their accounting expertise. Compliance with developing principles under Generally Accepted Accounting Principles (GAAP) requires a high level of specialized knowledge; the eight-hundred-page standards issued by the Financial Accounting Standards Board are beyond most in-house staffs. Such access could be purchased separately, but the seriousness of response is enhanced if the auditing firm is responsible for attesting to its correctness.

I had a related personal experience as the chief financial officer of a large mutual life insurance company in the 1960s. We were not required at that time to have our financial statements audited, and we elected not to do so. We relied on statutory accounting principles and the regulatory audits of the state insurance departments. This was the practice from the company's founding in 1933 until the first independent audit in 1969. That audit was done in order to comply with Securities and Exchange Commission requirements in connection with our issuing variable annuities, which the Supreme Court had recently determined to be investment securities as well as insurance contracts. To my knowledge, no inquiry or concern was ever raised by a policyholder, prospect, or regulator about our "unaudited" statements prior to that time.

In actual fact, we did use a public accounting firm extensively prior to auditing our statements, but only for their specialized knowledge. We sought their counsel on specific accounting and tax issues and for assistance in strengthening our internal accounting controls. We found the relationship quite satisfactory and useful. Once we switched them over to the usual requirements of the independent audit, our expense went up significantly, and the value of the relationship declined.

> *It is clear that the informed public—and, even more so, the uninformed public—expect the signature of the auditing firm to eliminate, not merely to reduce, what Professor Kinney calls "financial misstatement risk."*

It is clear that the informed public—and, even more so, the uninformed public—expect the signature of the auditing firm to eliminate, not merely to reduce, what Professor Kinney calls "financial misstatement risk." This expectation may not be reasonable, but it does exist. In effect, the litigation challenges to auditing firms make the accountants' opinion the equivalent of insurance, or a guarantee, that there is no financial misstatement.

There has been some discussion of formalizing the insurance aspect of financial misstatement risk.[1] Such an arrangement would involve an explicit guarantee by an insuring financial institution of the absence of financial fraud in corporate financial reports (with considerable complexity in defining just what that means). Risk premiums for such insurance would be established by underwriters as a cost variable depending on the company's misstatement risk profile and the reliance the insurer places on the independent audit—or, more likely, on the opinion of the auditor selected by the insurer.

[1] See the articles of Joshua Ronen, particularly "Post-Enron Reform: Financial Statement Insurance and GAAP Revisited," in "Enron: Lessons and Implications," special issue, *Stanford Journal of Law, Business, and Finance* 8, no. 1 (Autumn 2002): 39–68.

Perhaps the most interesting aspect of Professor Kinney's paper is his introduction of the two additional types of risk for which the public has apparently come to expect auditor responsibility: corporate business risk and corporate misconduct risk, which are covered by auditing professional standards only in extremis. If the auditor believes the firm may not survive, the "going concern" paragraph in the opinion gives a warning. But if a firm makes a risky acquisition, does the auditor have an obligation to report it beyond making sure the financial reporting reveals the risks? If a company provides executive compensation of extraordinary amounts, does the auditor have any reporting responsibility beyond being sure the board of directors has given proper approval? Although the general public may be outraged by high executive compensation, isn't this a question for boards rather than auditors?

I fully agree that we should focus strongly on strengthening the audit to prevent financial reporting fraud. The recent WorldCom and HealthSouth accounting frauds, for example—in amounts measured in the billions, where financial reports had been attested by the independent auditor—must raise fundamental questions about the adequacy and quality of Generally Accepted Auditing Standards (GAAS) or the auditors' fieldwork in applying them.

I am sure the senior managers of the four principal audit firms are examining their audit procedures. The new Public Company Accounting Oversight Board will be reformulating GAAS without the conflicted interests of auditors and preparers. Additionally, the forensic elements recommended for GAAS several years ago have been implemented recently. There is progress to report!

But all concerned with the quality of audits and the survival of the auditing profession in its present private form must focus on what Professor Kinney identifies as the first and traditional risk: that of financial misstatement.

Chapter 7

Professional Independence and the Corporate Lawyer

WILLIAM T. ALLEN AND GEOFFREY MILLER

Quickly following the shock and anger engendered by the collapse of the Enron Corporation came the accusations. Directed principally to the senior officers and auditors of the company, the accusations rippled out: "Where was the board?" "Where was the SEC?" As famously put by Judge Stanley Sporkin years earlier, when confronted with the evidence that Charles Keating had operated Lincoln Savings & Loan as a massive fraud, "Where were the lawyers?"

The charge against Enron's auditor was easy to grasp: Arthur Andersen's independence appeared to have been fatally infected, both by the huge audit fee that Enron generated and by the steady and substantial flow of nonaudit services. The auditor was seduced into complicity by large fees. Independence is the *sine qua non* of a public auditor, and when it is gone, the utility of the auditor's service dissipates.

Lawyers are different, and that difference has spared them from much of the criticism that has been directed at auditors. The core duty of a lawyer runs not to the public or to public markets but to the lawyer's client. The conception of the lawyer that dominates all others is that of the "zealous advocate." Under this ideal of undivided loyalty, the attorney is bound to defend the client with every legitimate means at his disposal. This conception of a lawyer's duty has powerfully beneficial social effects.

We value these benefits most keenly in the setting of a criminal prosecution. There the power of the state is arrayed against a single individual, and the liberty or even the life of that single person may stand in the balance. The ideal of pure and energetic loyalty originates with the lawyer in his role of defender of those under attack. As zealous advocates, lawyers are viewed in their most romantic and selfless state (John Adams defending British soldiers for acts at Bunker Hill; the heroic lawyers who stood against racial and ethnic prejudice in the Scottsboro Boys trial, or in the defense of the ill-fated Leo Franks).

But the mentality of the zealous advocate that inspires our admiration in some settings can lead to unprofessional conduct in others. In the litigation setting, the lawyer's imaginative arguments will be tested in a process that provides a range of counterbalances, from the discovery processes and cross-examination to informed counterarguments before a disinterested and expert arbiter. Removed from these safeguards and inserted into the process of the corporate lawyer in advising about prospective actions, this mentality can prove damaging to lawyer and client alike. To be sure, in giving such advice, lawyers are under an ethical constraint. An attorney may assist a client in carrying out a course of action that skirts the edge of the permissible only so long as the attorney believes in good faith that the action is, in fact, legally valid and the client is aware of the legal risks. The effectiveness of this restraint, however, depends largely upon the business lawyer's own willingness to make it effective. Therefore, the conditions under which the business lawyer practices are highly relevant to the profession's ability and willingness to act as a constraint on corporate clients' assuming unreasonable degrees of legal risk. There is good reason to believe that under the profession's present circumstances, busi-

▶ *The evolution of the legal profession over the last half century—from what we call a "club" form to a "market" form of organization—has produced conditions that have (1) atrophied the profession's acknowledgment of a duty to respect the discernible spirit animating the positive law and (2) reduced the leverage of practicing lawyers to influence their clients' willingness to assume unreasonable legal risks.*

ness lawyers—those who represented Enron, Worldcom, Tyco, HealthSouth, and their banks—have been forced by circumstances and the zeitgeist to take the narrowest possible zealous advocate view of their duty to the law itself.

We suggest that the evolution of the legal profession over the last half century—from what we call a "club" form to a "market" form of organization—has produced conditions that have (1) atrophied the profession's acknowledgment of a duty to respect the discernible spirit animating the positive law (for this is one way we articulate the duty of good faith) and (2) reduced the leverage of practicing lawyers to influence their clients' willingness to assume unreasonable legal risks. In this summary of a longer piece in process, we outline the changes in the environment that have produced these effects and suggest a few governance modifications, both in corporate clients' governance and in law firm organization, that may restore a bit of the lost ability of business lawyers to act with professional independence. It should be stated, however, that we do not intend for our generalizations concerning the effects of a changing environment on business lawyers' incentives to be understood as a charge against the moral character of business lawyers as a class.

FROM THE CLUB FORM OF ORGANIZATION TO MARKET COMPETITION

Subject to many qualifications to be treated elsewhere, we suggest that the club form of organization displays the following general features. First, significant social and legal barriers to entry produce a profession that is exclusive. Second, members often maintain social associations with one another and with clients outside their business relations. Third, competition is minimized, and when it occurs it is constrained by norms of politeness and courtesy. Fourth, the profession is marked by stable employment with little lateral mobility. Fifth, relations between lawyers and clients tend to be institutional and thus stable over time. Lastly, compensation for services is fixed in a flexible, not a mechanical, way (such as hours expended times a set hourly fee). If we imagine the legal profession circa 1950, it is easy to see each of these features of the club form of organization.

A critical feature of this world was the absence of a strongly competitive market for legal services. In this stable world, law firms had both economic and social levers to influence or constrain clients (or, more accurately, the officers who represented corporate clients). Economically, the deep knowledge that each law firm had concerning its client's business gave to each counseling firm a certain degree of market power vis-à-vis its client. Replacement would be cumbersome and costly. Socially, each officer of the firm, including the CEO, had had relations with the firm's lawyers for a significant period, starting in his training and junior years. In these relationships, dignity, respect, and trust were developed. Lawyers were not outside providers of commodity services. Of course, both of these sources of power could be used to extract economic rents, but they could also be used, if necessary, as a source of leverage in constraining a corporate officer who was willing to take excessive legal risk.

If we compare the characteristics of elite legal representation in the 1950s with the situation today, we observe a dramatic contrast in nearly all the elements that we have identified. The general paradigm for corporate practice has evolved from a club form of organization to a competitive form. From the huge growth in the number of lawyers (owing to a range of factors beyond the scope of this summary), to the removal of legal constraints on competition, to the emergence of national and international firms that engage in active marketing of services, the world of lawyers in private practice now looks radically different. Restraints on mobility have eased. Today it is not uncommon for attorneys to move from firm to firm several times during a career, sometimes taking clients with them.

Almost certainly, the most significant development respecting the ability of business lawyers to exercise constraining force on clients comes from the rationalization of the legal function within client firms and the development of large internal law departments. In a sense, the mission of the internal law department is to destroy the social and economic base that permitted outside counsel both to extract economic rents and to exercise useful constraint on aggressive corporate officers or employees. Internal law departments have this effect in a number of ways. First, lawyers (henceforth "outside" counsel) will be less likely to develop informal relations and the degree of trust and familiarity with senior officers that arose naturally under the prior system. (These relations may be replaced by inside lawyers, of course, but as we note below, these lawyers are structurally far less likely to constrain aggressive risk taking). Second, the informational advantage of counsel is diminished through a program of "spreading the work." This may arise as a method to control costs. Specialist firms and beauty contests appear. Because the charge is to monitor costs, corporate clients grow more price-sensitive and begin to demand closer supervision of charges for services. Competitive bidding for legal work comes onto the scene.

The evolution in the patterns within which business lawyers practice their profession has reduced their practical power to influence the conduct of their clients and has reduced, as well, their incentives to do so. The first result is a natural outgrowth of more competitive markets and is not the only effect of this change. In our longer paper, we will discuss how lawyers in the current environment may have less access to client information, may lack economic incentives to restrain clients or monitor others in the firm, and often face clients (officers and employees) with stronger incentives to "play for the sidelines" rather than "center court." The development of all of these points must await a fuller discussion.

CORPORATE LAWYERS' DUTY OF INDEPENDENCE

The foregoing points out some of the ways in which business lawyers and others who facilitate the design and effectuation of corporate transactions and disclosure have become less independent of their clients. This erosion in the external protections from client control and pressure can be expected to reduce the capacity and the willingness of corporate lawyers to act as an unwelcome constraint on the activities initiated by clients' officers. Such lawyers will tend, more likely, to comply with clients' wishes. Some may ask, "What is wrong with compliant lawyers, so long as they do not facilitate law breaking?" Ah, therein lies the rub. In a world in which all legal commands were unambiguous and all clients were motivated to obey the law, being a compliant lawyer would be an unalloyed virtue. But real life is complicated both by pervasive ambiguity in legal standards and by the existence of clients (or managing agents of clients) who sometimes seek to graze on pastures intended by lawmakers to be fenced off. In this world, a compliant lawyer can be an instrument of social injury. Thus, it is important that business lawyers recognize that the duty energetically to facilitate a client's lawful wishes must be supplemented with a duty, to the law itself, of independence. This is a duty to exercise independent (good faith) judgment concerning whether a proposed action falls within the law. We suggest that in representing clients in negotiating or structuring transactions, or in otherwise assisting clients in their ongoing efforts to do business within the law, lawyers are obliged to strive to advance, and not to thwart, the discernible spirit animating the law. The existence of an obligation to advance the discernible spirit that animates the law may seem controversial in some contexts. We leave for another day, or for other voices, the question of the duty of the lawyer conducting formal adversary proceedings, civil or criminal.

> ▶ *It is important that business lawyers recognize that the duty energetically to facilitate a client's lawful wishes must be supplemented with a duty, to the law itself, of independence. We suggest that in assisting clients in their ongoing efforts to do business within the law, lawyers are obliged to strive to advance, and not to thwart, the discernible spirit animating the law.*

STRENGTHENING THE PROFESSIONAL INDEPENDENCE OF CORPORATE LAWYERS: GOVERNANCE CONSIDERATIONS

The Role of the General Counsel

Corporations are the primary clients of corporate lawyers, and for most engagements a member of the internal legal team is the agent representing the client to the lawyer. Earlier, we cited the growth of large in-house legal departments as one of the signal developments that has reduced the leverage of private lawyers. The critical role played by inside lawyers today makes the incentives and controls of the inside general counsel and his or her staff highly salient to a consideration of the incentives facing practicing business lawyers.

In thinking about ways to enlist general counsel and internal lawyers in an effort to provide corporations with independent legal advice from outside corporate lawyers, we focus on three features of the general counsel's office: first, on the hiring, firing, and reporting process with respect to the general counsel personally; second, on the system of compensation of in-house lawyers; and, lastly, on the conception of the job. Slightly modifying existing practices along these lines would help to align the incentives of all general counsel with the long-term corporate interests of their firms, which we believe would, on balance, reduce excessive legal risk taking. Such general counsel would more likely adopt the norm that sees lawyers as agents seeking the realization of the spirit of the law.

Hiring, Firing, and Reporting of the General Counsel. Corporate governance principles and practices have not sufficiently focused on the critical role of the general counsel in assuring the corporation's compliance with law. Such attention would be less necessary in a world in which senior management of the enterprise had interests that were perfectly compatible with the long-term interests of the corporation. In fact, it is quite difficult to create management incentives that perfectly align these interests. Ordinarily, the CEO has incentives that are either oriented excessively toward risk avoidance (because his or her valuable human capital is invested solely in his or her employer) or oriented to excessive risk preference (due to substantial incentive compensation in the form of options that are more valuable the more volatile the stock, short of bankruptcy). This is, of course, a problem that can most effectively be dealt with through better design of incentive compensation programs. But for technical as well as political reasons, this is a difficult thing to do. In recent years, the dominant problem with senior management incentives appears to have been aggressive option compensation programs that created incentives for excessive risk taking or financial statement manipulation. Directors, on the other hand, rarely have significant incentive compensation. Thus, they have little or no economic interest in either taking on excessively risky projects or manipulating financial statements to pump up the stock price. From the point of view of incentives, the board is the better situated agency to assess risk policies of the firm. But boards have less relevant information than does the management team, usually less expertise, and certainly less time to evaluate courses of action.

As we focus our attention on the governance of legal risk, we see the same pattern. Senior management (when incented with options) has a greater incentive than the independent members of the board to allow financial statement "spin" or to "aggressively" manage earnings. Famously, in the late 1990s those incentives, coupled with dependent auditors infused with an advocacy mentality, produced massive manipulation. Congress's answer was to force boards to be more engaged and to try to shore up the independence of the professional advisors. A similar response is appropriate with respect to a risk of noncompliance with regulatory law.

While there are obvious and important differences, in some respects the general counsel can be analogized to the independent auditor. Every board of directors has a duty to exercise reasonable care to see that the corporation complies with the law.[1] The board may rely upon the CEO to assure compliance, but that reliance must be reasonable.[2] In our opinion, recognizing the inevitable imperfections in the incentive system facing the CEO, and the importance to the corporation that it take reasonable steps to be in compliance with the law, it ought not to be deemed satisfactory for the board to permit a CEO to act as its sole or primary channel of communication with the general

[1] *In re Caremark International, Inc. Derivative Litigation*, 698 A. 2d 959 (Del. Ch. 1996).
[2] See, e.g., 8 Del. C. Sec. 141.

counsel. Thus, direct contact and reporting from the corporation's chief legal officer is one way the board can show that it was appropriately active and informed in meeting this duty. An appropriate committee of the board should supervise the relationship between the general counsel and the corporation. This would entail being involved in hiring and firing decisions (e.g., conducting exit interviews) and exercising prudent oversight by direct, periodic communication with the general counsel. The appropriate board committee or lead director should insist upon direct and private access to the corporation's general counsel at any time and periodically.

Compensation of the General Counsel. Considered from a governance perspective, the corporate general counsel must be considered a lawyer first and a corporate officer second. Unless the general counsel is a competent lawyer, he or she cannot effectively fill the corporate office held. It is therefore the essence of the position that the general counsel exercise (or supervise an organization of lawyers who can be expected to exercise) legal judgment in a manner that reflects independent expert professional judgment. This is a difficult task, in part because inevitably the general counsel is a member of the management "team," and the familiar human instinct to cooperate will be felt by inside lawyers. This instinct, however, is often exacerbated by inclusion of the general counsel in option compensation programs. For this reason, it is unwise, in our judgment, to include general counsel in option compensation programs. Restricted stock grants are less problematic than options. *Ex post* bonus payments tied to measures unrelated to stock price would form a safer way to compensate unusually good performance, and would protect the general counsel to some extent from pressure to approve legally marginal strategies. Boards should impress on the general counsel his or her role as an independent force in the organization, responsive toward the corporate goals and plans determined by others, but responsible for law compliance to the board and his or her own independent professional judgment.

Conception of the General Counsel's Task. The board of directors should define the general counsel's charge, or pass upon the

CEO's charge to the general counsel. Of course, included within that charge should be the management of the corporation's costs of legal representation, but that ought not to be the central focus of the charge. Rather, the core responsibility of the inside legal department should be seen as providing reasonable assurance that the corporation is complying with applicable law, that its assets are appropriately protected, and that its rights are appropriately defended. Because of a series of dramatic events (moving at least from the Salomon Brothers treasury trading scandal through the charges of complicity in Enron's financial duplicity brought against Citigroup and J. P. Morgan Chase), the role of general counsel in financial institutions is coming to reflect a conception of the general counsel's mission in which supervising the firm's use of legal services is subsidiary to the overarching responsibility of assuring legal compliance with regulatory law and disclosure. Surely, the economical provision of these functions is an important feature of the general counsel's task; but just as the reduction of the independent auditor's fee is not the main mission of the audit committee, the general counsel's responsibilities extend far beyond minimizing the expense of legal counsel.

▶ *The core responsibility of the inside legal department should be seen as providing reasonable assurance that the corporation is complying with applicable law, that its assets are appropriately protected, and that its rights are appropriately defended.*

These corporate governance matters relate to our topic of lawyer independence in a rather obvious way. To the extent lawyers within firms are protected by boards from pressure to take overly aggressive legal positions when giving prospective legal guidance, there will be reduced pressure on outside corporate lawyers to do so as well.

The Organization of Law Firms

As we noted above, the characteristic setting for corporate lawyers in private practice today is the very large firm, offering a very broad range of legal services, with offices in many cities or countries. We have also noted the evolution of compensation structures in such firms. Often these firms must devise a system that attempts to gear compensation to individual productivity, somehow measured. And because the risks of such firms are difficult for individual lawyers to know about and to control, such firms permit individuals to protect themselves by adopting a limited liability structure for their participation.

Incentive Pay for Partners. Productivity-driven compensation always involves the problem of designing the incentives by selecting measures and according weights. When reasonably well designed, these are highly useful organizational tools. But they can never be perfectly designed. The more compensation is determined by some measure of individual productivity, the greater the reduction in the incentive for individuals to engage in activities that do not serve as markers of productivity. Thus, consulting with a partner about a difficult problem, which makes perfect sense when compensation is on a lockstep basis, may under an incentive compensation system look like a waste of time or a gift. It is striking that the modern firms with the greatest earnings per partner engage in little incentive compensation. In giving up some forms of incentives, they gain some measure of team involvement.

Incentive compensation within law firms often has another perverse consequence. As a partner's compensation depends more on his own production, his personal income will become less diversified (i.e., he will become more dependent on his client's fees). The resulting problem is particularly apparent when a lawyer spends most of his time on the work of a particular client. No matter what the firm's compensation practices, that lawyer will be under some additional pressure to keep that client happy. But that pressure will become intense in a system in which his compensation is directly tied in a material way to the fees that the lawyer produces. In that circumstance, given just the average amount of human weakness, such a lawyer's likelihood of trying, where appropriate, to constrain a very aggressive client will be markedly diminished. Incentive pay schemes for law partners are quite complex; in most instances, they risk reducing the professional independence of lawyers.

Limited Liability for Partners. Limited liability for lawyers is a modern innovation that both arises from and facilitates the growth of very large multicity law firms. If a firm is relatively small and located in only one city, monitoring of lawyers by their partners occurs more or less naturally and effectively. But if there are two or more degrees of separation between a partner in New York and a firm lawyer in London or Shanghai, it is quite easy to understand the incentive for partners to adopt a structure for their own participation that limits their vicarious liability. Allowing lawyers to protect their assets in this way, however, also reduces their incentives to see that other lawyers in the firm do not engage in liability-risking behavior. By reducing the incentive to monitor others, this structure in effect increases the risk that lawyers will allow themselves to be driven by client interests and demands to bless transactions or structures that violate the discernible spirit of law when a nonfrivolous account of compliance can be imagined.

Once a limited liability structure is adopted, the incentive for a lawyer to monitor the quality of the legal work of others in his or her office is reduced because he or she will be put at less economic risk by their actions. A lawyer protected by a limited liability structure would, of course, be exposed to loss caused by his own actions; but with respect to liabilities occasioned by the acts of another in the firm, his potential liability would be limited to his interest in the firm's assets. In most cases this will be a substantial and mind-concentrating loss—but it certainly will often be a substantial reduction from the partnership default of joint and several liability for all liabilities.

These are but a few of the concrete reforms that might be implemented to help guard against the risk that lawyers will sacrifice their professional independence in order to serve the short-term goals of high-ranking corporate officers, especially when those goals are at or beyond the line of the legally permissible. A number of other reforms are possible, but space does not permit us to explore them here. We plan to develop these ideas further in later work.

POSTSCRIPT: ON "THE DISCERNIBLE SPIRIT ANIMATING THE LAW"

Central to our notion that, in addition to their duties of confidentiality and zealous advocacy, lawyers should acknowledge and accept a duty to the integrity of the legal system itself, is the assertion that that duty may be adequately conceived as a duty to "the discernible spirit animating the law." But for legal positivists (which perhaps still means for most of us), the idea of employing such an obviously debatable, if not ephemeral, concept will be highly problematic. What can it mean? A spirit (perhaps even a discernible one) is obviously not something that can be objectified. It will often be the subject of honest debate. Does not the murkiness of this core idea mean that no actual system of professional self-regulation could incorporate such an obligation?

We do not think so. First, this concept is no less coherent than many legal doctrines usefully deployed every day in our legal order (consider "reasonable cause," for example, or "reasonable care"). Second, the search for the animating spirit of positive law (whether in statutes, regulation, or written contract) has long been conventionally understood as the guiding polestar of legal interpretation. Words themselves are imperfect and ambiguous symbols, and the human imagination that shapes them into legal commands is inevitably unable to foresee all of the contexts in which the problem addressed will later arise. Thus, as Learned Hand said many years ago in construing a statute, "There is no surer guide . . . than its purpose when that is sufficiently disclosed; nor any surer mark of oversolicitude for the letter than to wince at carrying out that purpose because the words do not formally quite match with it."[3]

Finally, criticism of the nonobjective nature of the discernible spirit standard would misunderstand the thrust of our suggestion. We do not suggest that business lawyers should be subject to sanction by licensing bodies for failure to counsel a client to comply with the discernible spirit animating applicable law. In this work, at least, we are concerned primarily with a profession-

---

[3] *Federal Deposit Insurance Corp. v. Tremaine*, 133 F.2d 827, 830 (2d Cir. 1943).

al's *self*-regulation, in the sense of individual professionals internalizing norms of behavior and regulating their conduct in accordance with such norms. In part, it is the power to control one's own actions that gives dignity to those activities that we deign to designate as professional undertakings. Thus, we have in mind a world in which business lawyers, in advising and assisting business clients to plan and accomplish transactions, ask themselves, and honestly answer for themselves, the question, "What is the purpose sought to be achieved by this (apparently ambiguous) regulatory scheme?" When a lawyer can discern with confidence the answer to that question, we suggest that he or she should feel bound by the professional norm of independence to advise the client accordingly and to limit his or her zealous advocacy.

Thus, for us, the fact that individuals—even those not driven by an advocacy mentality—might disagree about whether there is a "discernible spirit animating the law" in a particular setting is not problematic. For it is for individual business lawyers to make this determination and to be guided by it. What is required, in our view, is for the profession to acknowledge that to act in this way is consistent with the highest aspirations of the profession.

The Dubious History and Psychology of Clubs as Self-Regulatory Organizations

RICHARD W. PAINTER

You gentlemen are making a great mistake; the Exchange is a perfect institution.
  —Richard Whitney, president of the New York Stock Exchange, in 1934 Senate testimony opposing creation of the Securities and Exchange Commission[1]

I don't like academics sitting there speculating on what the ABA has or hasn't done....We're the lawyers, and we're the people who have been involved in the issue.
  —A. P. Carlton, president of the ABA, responding to law professors who supported federal regulation of securities lawyers[2]

Congress has for the first time put securities lawyers directly under the mandate of the Securities and Exchange Commission. Auditors are now regulated not only by the SEC but also by a new Public Company Accounting Oversight Board. The New

---

[1] Ron Chernow, *The House of Morgan: An American Banking Dynasty and the Rise of Modern Finance* (New York: Atlantic Monthly Press, 1990), 431.
[2] Renee Deger, "Law Professors Led Fight for New SEC Rules," *Recorder* (December 2, 2002).

York Stock Exchange is threatened with a drastic overhaul of its governance structure, and perhaps the loss of its status as a self-regulatory organization.

These changes are part of a seventy-year trend away from the "club system" (described in this volume by William Allen and Geoffrey Miller) and toward a larger, more diverse, and more tightly regulated financial services industry. Broker-dealers, accountants, and lawyers were once a club, or at least a group of clubs, almost entirely free of regulation from outside. Club members chose whom they wanted to be associated with, made their own rules, and relied on their own mechanisms to enforce those rules. From the 1930s on, however, federal regulation gradually brought the club system to an end.

▶ *While there may be other means of bringing transparency to financial markets besides increasingly stringent federal regulation of broker-dealers, auditors, and lawyers, a club system in which those professions are self-regulated by a cohesive group of insiders is probably not one of them. A look at the history of the club system indicates that it was effective at helping its members help themselves to large amounts of money.*

This essay draws on two areas of inquiry—history and psychology—to discuss whether the club system was ever an effective substitute for regulation of financial services, and to determine whether what remains of the club system has much to offer by way of self-regulation in the future. Both of those questions suggest that while there may be other means of bringing transparency to financial markets besides increasingly stringent federal regulation of broker-dealers, auditors, and lawyers, a club system in which those professions are self-regulated by a cohesive group of insiders is probably not one of them.

A look at the history of the club system indicates that it was effective at helping its members help themselves to large amounts of money. It was also effective, for a while, at excluding some individuals, principally because of ethnicity or religion, from access to certain relationships and the attendant financial rewards.

Anecdotal evidence from the history of major Wall Street law firms and brokerage houses suggests, however, that this system did little to improve standards of behavior:

David Dudley Field, founder of a firm that eventually became Shearman and Sterling, represented Jim Fisk and Jay Gould in their contest with Commodore Vanderbilt for control of the Erie Railroad in the 1870s. Both sides bribed New York judges, but Field claimed that he merely drafted the injunctions that corrupted judges signed, and that the bribery was thus not his responsibility.[3]

Elihu Root was the counsel of choice for Wall Street's financiers in the early 1900s— particularly for navigating around banking or antitrust laws. William Whitney perhaps best described Root's competitive edge: "I have had many lawyers who have told me what I cannot do. Mr. Root is the only lawyer who tells me how to do what I want to do."[4]

As President of the American Bar Association, Root led that organization in opposing the nomination of Louis Brandeis to the Supreme Court. Brandeis was the first Jew on the Court and was alleged to be insufficiently loyal to his moneyed clients. Furthermore, he had written a controversial book titled *Other People's Money and How the Bankers Use It.*[5]

William Nelson Cromwell of Sullivan & Cromwell persuaded Teddy Roosevelt's administration to buy the Panama Canal from his client, the French Canal Company. Colombian authorities in Panama, however, demanded too many concessions in return for permitting construction of the canal, making a revolution in Panama a condition precedent for closing the deal. Cromwell contacted Elihu Root, who had become Secretary of War, as well

[3] Richard W. Painter, "The Moral Interdependence of Corporate Lawyers and Their Clients," *Southern California Law Review* 67 (1994): 527–28.
[4] John T. Noonan, Jr., and Richard W. Painter, *Personal and Professional Responsibilities of the Lawyer*, 2nd ed. (New York, Foundation Press, 2001), 519.
[5] Louis D. Brandeis, *Other People's Money and How the Bankers Use It* (New York: Frederick A. Stokes, 1914), and Richard W. Painter, "Contracting Around Conflicts in a Family Representation: Louis Brandeis and the Warren Trust," *University of Chicago Law School Roundtable* 8 (2001): 353.

as other friends in Washington, so that appropriate arrangements could be made.[6]

Hoyt Moore of Cravath, Swaine & Moore represented Bethlehem Steel, which in the 1930s wanted control of the Williamsport Wire and Rope Company. After loaning large sums to Williamsport, Bethlehem threw the company into bankruptcy. Moore arranged to pay the bankruptcy judge, as well as the judge's sons, administrative fees, receivership fees and outright bribes, in return for which Williamsport was ordered to sell its assets to Bethlehem for a fraction of their worth. The judge, Albert Johnson of the Eastern District of Pennsylvania, was impeached, and Moore was implicated in a report of the United States Senate. Because the statute of limitations had run out, however, Moore was not indicted—and curiously, the bar did not impose professional discipline. The Cravath firm still bears his name, and his partner Robert Swaine heaped lavish praise on him in the firm's history. After two pages describing Moore's English and Scottish ancestry, his club memberships and his devotion to the firm (shown by his leaving at night after everyone else), Swaine got to the point: "No lawyer ever unreservedly gave more of himself to a client than Hoyt Moore has given to Bethlehem."[7]

Richard Whitney was the ultimate club man: educated at Groton School and Harvard College (Porcellian Club), treasurer of the New York Yacht Club, president of the New York Stock Exchange, and bitter opponent of the Securities Act of 1933 and Exchange Act of 1934. Later in the 1930s, Whitney got caught stealing not just from customers but also from the club itself. For using New York Yacht Club funds to cover his positions in the market, along with other crimes, he spent three years at Sing Sing, where he became captain of the baseball team. His former Groton headmaster, the Reverend Endicott Peabody, and friends from "the Porc" visited him there on weekends.[8]

[6] Richard W. Painter, "Moral Interdependence," 547.
[7] Robert Swaine, *The Cravath Firm and Its Predecessors* (New York: Ad Press, 1946), and Noonan and Painter, *Personal and Professional Responsibilities.*
[8] Chernow, *House of Morgan,* 421–29.

These are only a few examples, but history tells the same tale frequently: the club system was very adept at separating other people from their money.[9] Recommended reading includes Brandeis's book, as well as transcripts of the Pecora hearings, which Congress held before enacting the federal securities laws. Both describe failures of the club system in excruciating detail.

Economic self-interest and agency problems explain why participants in the club system acted to enrich themselves, and took advantage of investors who trusted them or their clients. It is clear that not all of this conduct was

▶ *Economic self-interest and agency problems explain why participants in the club system acted to enrich themselves, and took advantage of investors who trusted them or their clients.*

rational, however—particularly when one takes into account the fact that broker-dealers, lawyers, and auditors have always run the risk of public ire and government regulation.

The insights of cognitive psychology may explain the other part of this story: how a club system whose bedrock principle was self-regulation instead of government regulation, could at various points behave so foolishly that regulation from outside became inevitable. Cognitive biases thus may underscore at least some of the reasons why the club system, at its height in the 1920s, failed so miserably at preventing securities fraud. Cognitive biases also may help explain why the subsequent system of government-supervised self-regulation, undertaken at first instance by private organizations—whether the NYSE, the American Institute of Certified Public Accountants (AICPA), or the ABA—has been only partially effective and is once again vulnerable to being replaced by further direct government regulation.

Relevant biases include "cognitive conservatism" and "decision simplification," which cause decision makers to develop simplified explanations of occurrences, or schemas, resistant to evidence of change.[10] This tendency is exacerbated in group set-

[9] Brandeis, *Other People's Money.*
[10] These and other cognitive biases addresssed in this essay are discussed in Donald C. Langevoort, "Organized Illusions: A Behavioral Theory of Why Corporations Mislead Stock Market Investors (and Cause Other Social Harms)," *University of Pennsylvania Law Review* 146 (1997): 101, and Donald C. Langevoort, "Where Were

tings, where stress comes from challenging commonly held beliefs. Such stress is likely to be felt by an NYSE director who questions whether customers get the best price from a floor trading model, or by an AICPA member who questions whether nonaudit services improve audit quality, or by an ABA member who questions the association's interpretation of rules governing client confidences. Even more stress is imposed if leaders of these organizations can claim that tradition and "expert opinion" are on their side. Another bias, "overoptimism," arises from the tendency of organizations to promote an optimistic viewpoint in order to foster dedication and long-term commitment among their members, even though such a viewpoint may deflect evidence of negative developments (the Richard Whitney quote at the beginning of this essay, describing the NYSE as a "perfect institution" after the 1929 crash, is an excellent example). When there is sufficient ambiguity to allow it, people also sometimes infer "self-serving facts" that do not threaten their self-esteem or career prospects (e.g. the assertion that lawyers could not possibly have done anything wrong in the savings and loan crisis of the early 1990s). Finally, once a decision maker commits to a particular course of conduct, he or she may adhere consistently to that response ("commitment bias"), even if later confronted with evidence that the commitment was a bad choice. For example, a particular way of accounting for a transaction, once used by an issuer and blessed by its auditors, may be difficult for the issuer's managers and auditors to retreat from, even if evidence emerges to suggest that the accounting treatment was wrong.

Cognitive biases such as these are most potent when not open to challenge by outsiders with different perspectives. These outsiders, if given a chance to participate meaningfully in the club's decision making, might make a persuasive case that a particular approach is wrong, or that it is likely to trigger negative public reaction and may result in more direct government regulation. For example, the ABA's narrow interpretation of client communication rules led this author and other law professors to

the Lawyers? A Behavioral Inquiry into Lawyers' Responsibility for Clients' Fraud," *Vanderbilt Law Review* 46 (1993): 75.

propose first that the ABA change its rules, and then that the SEC or Congress impose "up-the-ladder" reporting requirements on securities lawyers.[11] Congress apparently also saw a side of the problem that the ABA did not when it enacted Section 307 of the Sarbanes-Oxley Act of 2002. The accounting industry's resistance in the 1990s to any SEC regulation of nonaudit services[12] set the industry up for the fall that came with Enron and WorldCom, which in turn triggered the far more draconian regulation imposed by Congress in 2002. Finally, the NYSE's insensitivity to how the public would view its chairman receiving almost a thousand times the pay of the SEC's chairman has not only brought about the resignation of an able leader from the Exchange; it may also bring about the diminishment of the NYSE's role as a self-regulatory organization. To the extent that cognitive biases promote "irrational" approaches to self-regulation by broker-dealers, auditors, and lawyers, an insular club system of self-regulation is probably less effective than a system that is open to broader public participation.

As Allen and Miller observe, there are positive aspects to the club system's use of reputation to regulate conduct—but, as they also note, these are no longer prevalent in a dispersed economy that is increasingly less reliant on repeat interaction among people who know each other. Furthermore, there is little historical evidence that the club system ever effectively regulated conduct that harmed anyone other than club members. Finally, reputational constraints on individual behavior were, and still are, outweighed by the psychological biases that flourish in an atmosphere where financial services professionals regulate themselves as would private clubs, oblivious to what is going on outside.

[11] Richard W. Painter and Jennifer E. Duggan, "Lawyer Disclosure of Corporate Fraud: Establishing a Firm Foundation," *Southern Methodist University Law Review* 50 (1996): 225. See also Painter et al., letter from twenty law professors to SEC chairman Harvey Pitt (March 7, 2002), http://www.fed-soc.org/Publications/practicegroupnewsletters/PG%20Links/pittletter.htm, and response from SEC general counsel David Becker (March 28, 2002), citing Painter and Duggan 1996, http://law.wustl.edu/Students/Courses/Seligman/AdvTopics2002/Materials/LetterFromDavidBeckerMarch28,2002.pdf.
[12] Arthur Levitt, *Take On the Street* (New York: Pantheon, 2002).

Chapter 8

The Financial Scandals and the Demise of the Traditional Investment Banker

FELIX G. ROHATYN

The recent financial scandals have badly damaged the credibility of American market capitalism and the trust in its main participants, raising serious concerns about the role of corporate directors, the integrity of auditors, the compensation of management, the functioning of commercial banks and investment banks, the responsibilities of law firms and credit-rating agencies, the role of regulators, and the responsibilities of the state and federal legislatures. All of these are related to each other, and the failure of any one weakens the financial system as a whole.

The failure of investment banks to maintain ethical and professional standards was rightly singled out as a major factor in these events. The criticism is justified, but closer scrutiny reveals an overlooked reality: what we call investment banks today bear no resemblance to what we knew as investment banks in the decades after World War II. The evolution of finance and of capital markets, the repeal of the Glass-Steagall Act, and the explosion in the technology of finance have totally changed the function of investment banks, which traditionally offered advice to corporations and protection to investors. Today's so-called investment banks bear no more relationship to their predecessors than yesterday's family doctors bear to HMOs.

Traditional investment banks provided advice to their corporate clients. Their senior partners often sat on the boards of these client companies. The banks organized the distribution of the corporate securities to the public, and their reputation and the long-term nature of their relationship constituted a "seal of approval" for the benefit of the public. The investment banker felt responsible for the quality of the securities offered to the public and was often a long-term investor in the companies he represented. Investment banks were relatively small partnerships, headed by prestigious individuals whose reputations stood behind their firms.

The evolution of the financial markets and changes in the regulatory climate have eliminated the differences between the functions of commercial banks and investment banks. Investment banks no longer invest; they sell products. They trade for their own account, as do commercial banks, whether in derivatives, foreign exchange, or securities; many have become large hedge funds. They are large public corporations, in lieu of small partnerships, with priority given to their own stock price instead of the representation of their clients. Investment banks compete vigorously with commercial banks for the highly profitable mergers and acquisitions advisory business, providing easy credit and favorable stock coverage by their institutional analysts. Their "traditional relationship" with corporate clients and investors has all but disappeared. Today's investment bankers shop their services to the best bidder.

▶ *The repeal of the Glass-Steagall Act has opened a Pandora's box of myriad conflicts. It is hard to see how to unscramble the omelet. Ethics cannot be legislated, but they can be rewarded by the marketplace or punished by the courts.*

When it comes to underwriting securities and protecting the public, the requirement of "full disclosure" has been superseded by disclosure so massive and detailed that no one but specialists can begin to understand the facts. The most prestigious and respected financial publications, in commenting on the recent scandals, argued that "caveat emptor" should be the rule of the marketplace and that investors have mostly themselves to blame. This is surely not what the framers of the 1933 and 1934 securities acts had in mind. Conflicts of interest are rampant—between the role of principal and the role of advisor, between the role of underwriter and the allocation of "hot" initial public offerings, and between the role of research as a corporate business-getting function and the role of research as a service to the investing client.

The absence of investment bankers on corporate boards, while following the rules of independence currently urged on corporate America, removes the influence of sophisticated, influential leaders of the financial community from these boards. Their reputations and their capital would be at risk if they had willingly allowed the kind of excesses we have witnessed recently. It is hard to imagine a Morgan, a Schiff, or a Lehman voting to suspend the ethics code of a corporation on whose board he sat.

The repeal of the Glass-Steagall Act has opened a Pandora's box of myriad conflicts. It is hard to see how to unscramble the omelet. Ethics cannot be legislated, but they can be rewarded by the marketplace or punished by the courts. Corporate America and institutional investors can support ethical and traditional investment bankers with their business. Firms that would limit their activities to corporate advice, asset management, and principal investing would recapture their importance and attract the best and the brightest young bankers. The courts and the regulators should crack down on egregious cases of conflicts of interest, failure to meet fiduciary obligations, abuse of inside information, and other types of legal and ethical lapses. Not only should the culpable firms be punished; the individuals involved should be also sanctioned, just as lawyers are disbarred and doctors lose their licenses.

It must also be recognized that the demise of the traditional investment banker was accelerated by changes in corporate America and by the increased power of the big company chief financial officer (CFO) in an increasingly complicated financial environment. As a result of the greater complexity of the system and the treatment of the financial function as a profit center, the

CFO took on more and more of the functions previously shared by the CEO and the investment banker, whose relationship became secondary—and the commercial banks, helped by the repeal of the Glass-Steagall Act, played a more and more pervasive role. Both for banks and investment banks, finance became increasingly a product to be manufactured as well as to be bought and sold. In combination with compliant lawyers and auditors, this led straight to the scandals recently revealed.

It is impossible today to distinguish commercial banks from investment banks, especially the very large ones. However, it is possible to distinguish among the ethical cultures promoted by various firms and their leaders. Every year a list of the most admired companies is published; similarly, a prestigious independent board could be created to nominate the five most reputable investment banks. It would not take long for corporate boards to encourage relationships with the best and avoid the others. The marketplace would do the rest, and tax avoidance schemes, accounting scams, and self-serving and false recommendations would soon lose their appeal.

Toward A Higher Standard of Conduct in Investment Banking

GERALD ROSENFELD

There are many complexities to the role of the investment banker in the recent corporate scandals. Indeed, as Felix Rohatyn points out, even the definition of an investment banker is complex in today's world. There is, however, a more straightforward aspect of this issue, and it relates to the realm of markets and economics—the world in which investment bankers live.

We have ample evidence, going back many decades, that aberrational market periods provide fuel for scandal. Indeed, it was the Roaring Twenties that led us to create the Glass-Steagall separation of lending and underwriting, which created investment banking in the first place. More recently, there have been three extensive scandals involving investment bankers in the past twenty years: the insider trading scandals of the mid-1980s, the junk bond scandals of the early 1990s, and the more recent equity research scandals. Each came at the end of an extreme period of growth in the related markets.

Specifically, after being reasonably constant for a decade, U.S. merger and acquisition activity went from $58 billion in 1982 to the previously unimagined level of $353 billion in 1987.[1] The huge volume of merger arbitrage opportunities thus created provided the fuel that was to be ignited by the spark of immoral

---

[1] Data provided by Thomson Financial, May 9, 2003.

and illegal behavioral tendencies among some investment bankers and traders. A similar phenomenon occurred in the high-yield ("junk") bond market in the late 1980s. The non-investment-grade bond market bumped along at under $2 billion of primary issuance for a number of years until 1981, growing in a three-year period to $11 billion in 1984, $15 billion in 1985, and $31 billion in 1986. It remained above $24 billion for the rest of the decade before coming to a crashing halt in the scandals of 1990–91, involving investment bankers, savings and loan executives, insurance companies, and other money managers.[2] Again, an aberrational market period provided the fuel for an outburst of bad behavior.

▶ *When an investment banker can earn a lifetime's worth of compensation—or ten lifetimes' worth—in one or two years of extreme markets, the pressure on behavior is sometimes too great to bear.*

Consider, then, the equity markets of the late 1990s. Primary issuances (IPOs) soared from $5 billion in 1990 to $63 billion in 1999,[3] while the total value of the U.S. equity market reached $18 trillion in 1999 after being below $5 trillion as late as 1994.[4] Here was the fuel, but where the spark? As Felix indicates, the confusion of roles taken on by financial service professionals—from lender to underwriter, from advisor to investor—created so much conflict that any tendency toward unethical behavior found ample opportunity to manifest itself. It is also not surprising that equity research became another friction point that enabled scandal to develop. (I expand on this point below.)

Thus, the straightforward part of the investment banker's role in the corporate scandals is encapsulated in the answer that Willy Sutton, the bank robber, gave when asked why he robbed banks: "It's where the money is." Scandal goes where the money is—particularly in aberrational markets, where market participants, whether consciously or subliminally, are trying to "get it

---

[2] Data provided by Thomson Financial, May 12, 2003.
[3] Data provided by Thomson Financial, May 13, 2003.
[4] Securities Industry Association, *Securities Industry Fact Book 2001* (New York: Securities Industry Association, 2001), 48.

while [they] can." When an investment banker can earn a lifetime's worth of compensation—or ten lifetimes' worth—in one or two years of extreme markets, the pressure on behavior is sometimes too great to bear.

Nor is it surprising that one of the investment banker's conflict roles in the recent scandals arose around equity research. Indeed, Wall Street or "sell-side" research has undergone such a fundamental change in its economic basis as to call into question its continued existence. At its beginnings, sell-side research was an adjunct to the salesmen and traders at brokerage firms, providing insight and analysis to (mostly) institutional investors in exchange for those investors' buying and selling through the investment bank. With pre-1975 fixed commissions of as much as 30 cents per share, there was enough economics to compensate salesmen, traders, and research analysts, albeit at relatively modest levels. With fixed commissions undone in 1975, and with the increasing power of large institutional investors in the market, commissions fell to under five cents per share. Research had no place to go for its economic backing, other than to investment banking.

In truth, sell-side research has been an arm of, and financially supported by, investment banking for more than two decades, not just for the past few years. It was only the aberrational markets of the late 1990s that brought research analysts, their role, and their compensation to the front line of the scandals. With hundreds of millions of fee dollars available to investment banks for IPOs, the temptation to use sell-side analysts as marketing tools and the ability to pay them tens of millions in compensation finally revealed the perversion of the research role.

With this in mind, the future of sell-side research is in doubt. Who will pay for this service? Institutional investors who mostly do their own "buy-side" research are glad to receive sell-side research for free but won't support it economically. Retail investors, whom the press portrays as having been betrayed by analysts, will not see their transaction costs increased to pay for research. Investment banking departments will still support research only if fees can be attributed to its presence. So-called independent research firms will find it difficult to generate enough fees to pay for quality people after the current flurry of activity around research conflicts has died down. Thus, research will return to being an adjunct of investment banking (although less visible and more carefully monitored than before), or it will be a public relations loss leader for very large companies like Citigroup, or it will effectively disappear.

Finally, we come to the question of whether investment banking is (or should be) recognized as a profession with obligations to the public interest, including responsibility as a "gatekeeper" helping to constrain corporate misconduct. A dictionary definition of *profession* is "an occupation requiring extensive training." I know of no specific criteria that one must meet to be called an investment banker. In the sense of the term used in this discussion, training is clearly required, but it is nowhere near as formal as the training and certification associated with, say, a lawyer or a CPA. One potential improvement might be to require some form of standard examination or certification for investment bankers.

There is no code of conduct established specifically for investment banking. Investment bankers are simply expected to obey the law. In their role as underwriters, the 1933 and 1934 securities acts are relevant. In their role as broker-dealers, they must follow the rules of the National Association of Securities Dealers and other self-regulatory agencies. In their role as merger advisors, they must observe insider trading rules. But no specific body of behavioral rules is associated with the investment banking "profession." Indeed, as Felix notes, the conflict of roles and the investment bankers' positions as high-level employees of their own public corporations has led to the very behaviors we have observed. Whether some investment bankers have violated civil rules or even criminal statutes during the recent scandals will become known over time, as cases are adjudicated. Undoubtedly, some clarifications—and possibly some reinterpretations—of existing laws and civil rules will come out of this period. Perhaps the investment banking community should adopt and try to enforce its own code of conduct and ethics. We might require the teaching of this code in all internal training programs at investment firms.

What is to be learned from the investment banker's role in the recent scandals? A few thoughts emerge. Although ethical behavior can't be legislated, we can be alert to the increased pressures on behavior in extraordinary times. A higher level of alertness on the part of regulators and senior managers in financial services during such times might have prevented some of the excesses of the past, and might prevent some during the next aberrational period. The gradual blurring of traditional investment banking business with lending and other principal activities was clearly a source of conflict that sparked the problems. Perhaps a clearer set of separation structures (but probably not a new Glass-Steagall) would help. It does seem clear, though, that external forces, both market and regulatory, will continue to pressure investment bankers toward higher standards of conduct—and that the investment banking community would do well to try to put its own house in order.

Journalists and the Corporate Scandals: What Happened to the Watchdog?

GENEVA OVERHOLSER

The press has an acknowledged responsibility to protect the public interest by reviewing and disclosing corporate misconduct. The recent surge of scandals made clear that the media frequently fail in that responsibility. There are several reasons why—and some evident possibilities for addressing the shortcomings.

THE NATURE OF THE BUSINESS WORLD

For journalists, the business world's lack of transparency, compared with the relatively high transparency of the world of government and politics, poses a particular challenge. "It's harder to do business reporting," says Martha Steffens, the SABEW (Society of American Business Editors and Writers) Chair in Business and Financial Journalism at the Missouri School of Journalism. "They don't have to give you the information."[1] Indeed, corporations often go to considerable lengths to keep information private—or to obfuscate when making information public. In a 1994 Freedom Forum report on media-corporate

---

[1] Telephone conversation with the author.

relations, 70 percent of business leaders acknowledged being neither candid nor truthful with journalists.[2]

Also complicating coverage of business is a lack of clarity about standards in the business world. A recent *New York Times* book review, "Business Ethics and Other Oxymorons," notes "the casual way corporate America has often viewed ethical issues."[3] If it's hard to judge an ethical lapse even from inside a corporation, doing so from outside is hard indeed, particularly at today's pace of change. Kim Clark, dean of the Harvard Business School, said in a recent National Press Club speech that all, "including the media," must help restore faith in the business system. Values like right and wrong "are taught at home, in your family, in your early experiences," Clark said.[4] But the degree to which these values are observed—and observable—in corporate America is not so clear.

In addition, there is a certain deferential diffidence within the business culture, one corporation to another—and the media are themselves, for the most part, businesses. This tends to restrain the assertiveness of business reporting, as well as to drive it toward the positive.

THE NATURE OF BUSINESS REPORTING

For all the challenges posed by the culture of American business, the culture of business reporting is the central problem. The overriding issue is what Steffens, the business journalism professor, calls "the talent level." Business reporting, she says, is "less sexy" than other beats. "It's much easier to save lives than to be the protector of someone losing $50,000 on the market."[5] A 2002 American Press Institute (API) *Business Journalism Survey* made clear just how low the status of business journalism is—in

[2] Mike Haggerty and Wallace Rasmussen, *The Headline vs. the Bottom Line: Mutual Distrust Between Business and the News Media* (Nashville: Freedom Forum, 1994).
[3] Floyd Norris, "Business Ethics and Other Oxymorons," *New York Times,* April 20, 2003.
[4] Kim Clark, "Corporate Scandals: Is It a Problem of Bad Apples, or Is It the Barrel?" (speech, National Press Club, Washington, DC, February 26, 2003).
[5] Telephone conversation with the author.

the business community, in journalism education, and particularly within the newsroom: "When compared to other desks in the newsroom, business desks are deemed the least talented, by far." In addition, "Business is the lowest priority for current resources in the newsroom by a large margin." [6] With resources in the average American newsroom increasingly squeezed by profit pressures, this leaves many business-section resources pinched indeed.

In a business in which lack of training is endemic—it's widely cited as a primary source of staff dissatisfaction—the business desk is even worse off than others. Few journalism schools have a strong business emphasis. And as business is not typically covered in university newspapers, student journalists don't learn business reporting "on the job." To add to the problem, innumeracy and a downright fear of numbers plague many journalists. Brant Houston, director of the nonprofit organization Investigative Reporters and Editors, says business reporters are now "receiving more training on documents and databases, but they still don't get sufficient time to probe businesses that have questionable practices. In addition, business *editors* need more training in order to do more watchdog work."[7]

Of course, the media are no monolith. Whereas the business sections of many small newspapers are essentially press release publishing services, business leaders surveyed by API scored the large national newspapers quite high on business coverage. Television, meanwhile, scored very low. But there are beat-structure issues that tend to weaken the reporting even in strong business news organizations. A Reuters reporter told me that her colleagues are selective about their beats: "They don't want to cover the SEC. They want IMF, the World Bank, Greenspan. The regulatory stuff is tedious." This leaves lesser talents to work on beats where corporate misconduct is likeliest to be discovered. And all too often, said the Reuters reporter, "They wait for a press release, call a couple of people, and get out the story."

---

[6] American Press Institute, *Business Journalism Survey,* July–August 2002.
[7] E-mail exchange with the author.

Similarly, the financial press is set up to cover the financial markets—"but CEOs who get paid too much? That's no one's beat."[8]

One symptom of the low level of talent is the prevailing tendency to be reactive rather than to pursue the assertive watchdog approach more common to political journalism. Indeed, investigative reporter Steve Weinberg, a biographer of Armand Hammer, says it is not lack of business world transparency but lack of business journalism vigor that holds the media back. "Journalists aren't thinking about how to find the good stories before the SEC issues a press release or an attorney files a class-action suit on behalf of the stockholders," he says. "Journalists can do this work. Especially with public corporations, there's so much stuff on file—and even with private corporations, if you know where to look."

▶ *In the go-go climate of 1999–2000, journalists were as irrationally exuberant as anyone. No longer critics, they became players—even cheerleaders.*

Weinberg continues, "It never occurs to business leaders that there are all these documents out there that could hang them. It never occurs to them that journalists might actually find that stuff, because journalists usually don't. So the moguls have developed this way of thinking that nobody is going to hold them accountable, and most of the time they are right."[9] Thus, the corporate scandals piling up in recent years have left many—even insiders—shocked. "My sense among regulators and prosecutors is that we're all rather surprised as to how much fraud is out there," the president of the North American Securities Administrators Association told the *New York Times* recently.[10]

A further problem concerns the viewpoint of business reporting. Interestingly, recent events have turned on its head a traditional criticism of business reporting: the view, long held by business executives, that reporters were reflexively anti-business. In 1997 Bill Cooper, chair and CEO of Minneapolis-based TCF Financial Corporation, said at a conference that "the people

[8] Private conversation with the author.
[9] Telephone conversations with the author.
[10] Alex Berenson, "A U.S. Push on Accounting Fraud," *New York Times*, April 9, 2003.

doing the business writing have an attitude about business. Most think business is bad." Local media coverage is "voyeuristic, looking for nasty little stories and sensationalism without a lot of thought to the consequences."[11]

Now the opposite charge carries more weight. In the go-go climate of 1999–2000, journalists were as irrationally exuberant as anyone. No longer critics, they became players—even cheerleaders, as Howard Kurtz notes in his book on that era, *The Fortune Tellers:* "The media act as a great seducer ('The Best Mutual Funds!' 'Secrets of the Stock Stars!'), luring people to tune in or log on or open their checkbooks on the promise of major paydays to come."[12] Former executive Gerald Levin, expanding on this theme, told me, "I believe that there has been a singular lack of financial sophistication in the business press, where fads and trends prevailed instead of skeptical questioning. It is also my view that the general press failed to raise issues of morality and character in covering corporate executives. There was too much focus on personalities, power and money—the wrong form of idolatry."[13] Jane Bryant Quinn, in the 1998 *Columbia Journalism Review* article "When Business Writing Becomes Soft Porn," said, "In the 1980s, we embarrassed ourselves by falling in love with corporate raiders. In the '90s, we're panting after stock pickers, photogenic mutual-fund managers and billionaires. We obviously have to cover these people, but too many stories read as if they were written for fan magazines."[14] And Jeffrey Madrick wrote in the *Nieman Reports* (Summer 2002), "There's been no golden age in financial journalism, but in earlier times there did seem to be some sense of proportion. But during this past decade, proportion wasn't what got reporters far with many editors of the financial news."[15]

[11] Patricia Hedberg. "Is the Media Just Another Business?" (Stakeholder Dialogue, "The Media and Business: A Rocky Relationship," University of St. Thomas in Minneapolis, Spring 1997).
[12] Howard Kurtz, *The Fortune Tellers* (New York: Touchstone, 2000).
[13] E-mail exchange with the author.
[14] Jane Bryant Quinn, "When Business Writing Becomes Soft Porn," *Columbia Journalism Review,* March/April 1998.
[15] Jeffrey Madrick, "A Good Story Isn't Always the Right One to Tell," *Nieman Reports* 56, no. 2 (Summer 2002): 7.

It is important to note the broader question of professionalism as regards journalism generally. Journalists are hesitant to refer to their line of work as a profession, and for good reason. There is no accreditation process, no exam to be passed, no degree required. There are no universal standards, no industry-wide code of ethics. There is no inclusive national organization, no board of overseers, and no agreed-upon process of discharge or reprimand, short of libel law. Individual media draw up individual answers: codes of ethics, corrections policies, ombudsmen and reader advisory councils, a few city or state press councils. Attempts at broadening or standardizing such practices run up against both the fact of media fragmentation and the deeply held conviction that press freedom would thereby be fettered. Concern about press standing today has raised support for stronger answers than those currently in place. But the marks of true professionalism do not appear on the horizon.

YET GOOD REPORTING HAPPENS—CREATING FURTHER CHALLENGES FOR THE JOURNALIST

Amid the rush of critics who have derided the press's failure to tell the stories of corporate misconduct before the government found it, the *Wall Street Journal*'s managing editor, Paul Steiger, cries foul. Certainly, the Pulitzer for explanatory reporting this year—awarded "to the *Wall Street Journal* Staff for its clear, concise and comprehensive stories that illuminated the roots, significance and impact of corporate scandals in America"—highlights reporting that will be useful to those watching out for the next round of misconduct. But Steiger goes further. In the *Nieman Reports* (Summer 2002), he asserted that the Enron scandal "was actually uncovered by the relentless, careful, intelligent work of two *Wall Street Journal* reporters."[16]

If there are strong exceptions to the negative image of business reporting, the hard, digging business reporting that does get done can create its own challenges. For one thing, the public

[16] Paul Steiger, "Not Every Journalist 'Missed' the Enron Story," *Nieman Reports* 56, no. 2 (Summer 2002): 10.

may not want to hear it. Much as the wartime media suffer from criticism of their failures of patriotism, critical business reporting is charged with being anticapitalist—even downright un-American. Americans like business success—and many of them very much like business executives, too. I discovered this when I wrote occasional columns about the excesses of corporate compensation packages and the growing gap between the very rich and the very poor. These elicited stinging responses: I was fomenting class warfare. I was failing to appreciate the irreplaceable—even unchallengeable—talents of America's CEOs.

That, however, was several years ago. In April 2003, writing in her *New York Times* Market Watch column, Gretchen Morgenson noted, "In the 1990s, corporate executives were allowed to siphon off so much shareholder wealth for so long that it seems some of them still cannot see why shareholders—the true owners—are finally taking issue with their grasping ways."[17] The executives' surprise is understandable; although there was considerable reporting on this particular form of corporate excess, many people simply didn't want to hear it.

Then, of course, there are the much more dramatically *negative corporate responses* to effective business reporting. The tale of *Fortune*'s Bethany McLean is familiar. When she questioned Enron's Jeffrey Skilling, he called her questions "unethical" and hung up on her. Then Enron chairman Ken Lay called one of her editors to try to get the story spiked. Many an effective reporter has been denied access to a corporation's executives after the publication of unwelcome stories. And then there is Gannett's $14 million settlement over its 1998 *Cincinnati Enquirer* investigation of Chiquita Brand's business practices. The *Enquirer*'s reporting included illegal e-mail accessing. Yet, as SABEW's Steffens said, "Never to this day has anyone ever questioned any fact in that story." Nevertheless, she noted, "there was clearly a chilling effect. When [millions of dollars are] so quickly upcoming from a corporate parent. . . .Who could put their company at that kind of financial risk by going after a local com-

[17] Gretchen Morgenson, "Boldly Defending Their Options in a Penitent Age," Market Watch, *New York Times,* sec. 3, April 20, 2003.

pany with endless resources, endless PR, endless lawyers? It's a lot easier to go up against open records, or against a senator—they're not going to sue you."[18]

STILL, THERE'S HOPE

Despite all these challenges, many observers feel that business reporting is better than it's ever been. That's partly a matter of growth. In 1997 Deborah Howell, chief of the Washington bureau for the Newhouse Newspaper Group and editor of the Newhouse News Service, noted, "The newspaper business is so much better at covering business than we were 20 years ago." Newspaper business sections have "more space, more reporters, more education of the reporters, and better daily and Sunday sections."[19]

▶ *Training is critically needed. In an era of increasing dominance by business, journalism schools need to incorporate business journalism into their government-dominated curricula, particularly in investigative reporting.*

In addition, the big scandal stories have goaded business reporters into more activism. Says IRE's Houston, "I think the quality of reporting on corporate misconduct has improved significantly."[20] Reporters have learned that the blind trust—and, indeed, the celebrity hunt—were unwarranted and even harmful.

Another piece of good news is that Americans care more about business reporting than ever. As one of my graduate students wrote in her thesis: "We're in a new era when business news is no longer relegated to the back of the sports page, and ordinary Americans not only read/watch it but act and depend on it. That's a boon . . . to media outlets and to the journalists themselves but with it comes new responsibility and scrutiny. Good business journalism simply matters more now."[21]

[18] Telephone conversation with the author.
[19] Hedberg, "Is the Media Just Another Business?"
[20] E-mail exchange with the author.
[21] Kate Miller, "The Industry Standard in Washington: Covering the New Economy in Transition" (master's thesis, Missouri School of Journalism, 2001).

RECOMMENDATIONS FOR IMPROVEMENT

Training is critically needed. Business journalists need ongoing training on how to review the documents and databases that hold warning signs of corporate misconduct. In an era of increasing dominance by business, journalism schools need to incorporate business journalism into their government-dominated curricula, particularly in investigative reporting. And newsroom executives must ensure that resources—not only training but also salaries, travel money, "newshole," and reporter time—are directed more equitably toward this increasingly important part of the news organization.

The mission of business reporting needs clarifying and strengthening. Editors who put their best reporters on government beats and prod them to be aggressive need to ask themselves why they do so much less on the business desk. Weinberg proposes replacing "business reporting" with "investigative reporting of the private sector—a whole different tone. It conveys anticipating instead of reacting. It conveys looking at all the players instead of just the CEO. We need to talk to labor leaders, to workers, to board members."[22]

The focus, moreover, must be turned toward the press's responsibility to the public—as investors, as residents of a community, as citizens of a democracy. Insider perspectives won't suffice; in an era when more and more invest, financial education is a necessary component of business reporting. And boosterism must give way to careful, fair-minded, comprehensive scrutiny. Business reporters must be constantly mindful that their loyalty is to readers (or viewers or listeners). Writes columnist Quinn: "In many ways, the personal finance press covers a world of predators and prey. We're supposed to stick up for the prey. Who will defend them, if not us? Yet we tend to dine with the predators. . . . They're the force field."[23]

Greater transparency is badly needed in the American business world. As Steffens notes, business journalists are writing

---

[22] Telephone conversation with the author.
[23] Quinn, "When Business Writing Becomes Soft Porn."

about emerging markets, and one of the tenets is the need to move toward transparency. "How transparent are American markets?" she asks. With increasing amounts of foreign money in American stock exchanges, "If we in journalism don't do our jobs, and the markets aren't transparent, the market valuation is going to decline. If people don't think companies here are operating honestly, it might be our fault as journalists. If we did our jobs better, it might make a difference."[24] Those should be grounds on which business leaders and business journalists could begin to work together for improvement.

▶ *A final and, indeed, overarching challenge stems from the conduct of media executives today. The extraordinary pressure brought to bear on newsgathering organizations—by corporations seeking to improve their profit margins, quarter by quarter; by executive compensation plans that reward short-term success; and by the primacy of shareholder interests—is steadily undermining the ability of the press to serve the needs of democracy.*

This transparency must begin at home. Media leaders, ironically, tend to be even less forthcoming than their peers in other businesses. Even as their own organizations push for openness from others, media executives hold financial information exceptionally close to the vest. This must change. Media executives can create greater confidence in the concept of openness by leading the way toward a culture of business transparency.

A final and, indeed, overarching challenge stems from the conduct of media executives today. The extraordinary pressure brought to bear on newsgathering organizations—by corporations seeking to improve their profit margins, quarter by quarter; by executive compensation plans that reward short-term success; and by the primacy of shareholder interests—is steadily undermining the ability of the press to serve the needs of democracy. The value of the newspaper to its community, its responsibilities to its employees and consumers, and its resources for research and investment, training and salaries, newsprint and circulation efforts—all these are much affected by the business practices of publicly held media companies, and by the coming together of

[24] Telephone conversation with the author.

America's media organizations into fewer and fewer corporate hands—but that is a matter for another discussion (indeed, it is a story sorely undertold, for few in the media are eager to tell it). Also, the effect of the remarkable levels of media profitability is enormous, and certainly pertinent to the issue at hand.

Joseph Pulitzer, when he made his proposal to found the Columbia Graduate School of Journalism, wrote, "Our Republic and its press will rise or fall together. An able, disinterested, public-spirited press, with trained intelligence to know the right and courage to do it, can preserve that public virtue without which popular government is a sham and a mockery. A cynical, mercenary, demagogic press will produce in time a people as base as itself. The power to mold the future of the Republic will be in the hands of the journalists of future generations."[25] The warning is timely. When journalism takes a distant back seat to profitability, the press is a poor watchdog against business *or* government.

[25] Joseph Pulitzer, "The College of Journalism," *North American Review* (May 1904).

PART III

Report of the American Academy's Corporate Responsibility Steering Committee

CORPORATE RESPONSIBILITY STEERING COMMITTEE
OF THE
AMERICAN ACADEMY OF ARTS AND SCIENCES

Martin Lipton *(co-chair)*
Wachtell, Lipton, Rosen & Katz

Jay W. Lorsch *(co-chair)*
Harvard Business School

Larry Sonsini *(co-chair)*
Wilson Sonsini Goodrich & Rosati

William T. Allen
New York University Center for Law
& Business

Leslie Berlowitz
American Academy of Arts and
Sciences

John H. Biggs
TIAA-CREF (retired)

Margaret M. Blair
Vanderbilt University Law School

Richard Buxbaum
Boalt Hall School of Law
University of California, Berkeley

Alfred D. Chandler
Harvard Business School (emeritus)

James Cochrane
New York Stock Exchange, Inc.
(retired)

Michael E. Gellert
Windcrest Partners

Amory Houghton, Jr.
United States House of
Representatives

Rakesh Khurana
Harvard Business School

Douglass C. North
Washington University-St. Louis

Geneva Overholser
University of Missouri School of
Journalism

John S. Reed
Citigroup Inc. (retired)

Mark J. Roe
Harvard Law School

Felix G. Rohatyn
Rohatyn Associates LLC

Gerald Rosenfeld
Rothschild North America

E. John Rosenwald, Jr.
Bear, Stearns & Co. Inc.

Damon Silvers
AFL-CIO

Michael Useem
The Wharton School
University of Pennsylvania

Andy Zelleke
American Academy of Arts and
Sciences

Report of the American Academy's Corporate Responsibility Steering Committee

The early years of the new century have been plagued by major scandals at Enron and WorldCom, by numerous instances of overly aggressive accounting and excessive executive compensation, by compromised auditors and securities analysts, by inattentive boards of directors, and by self-indulgent mutual fund managers. Public confidence in American business and finance has been shaken to a degree not seen since the Great Depression. Just as the Depression ushered in a period of intense reform, recent scandals have produced the Sarbanes-Oxley Act of 2002, new rules at the stock exchanges, a more vigilant Securities and Exchange Commission, and reenergized state attorneys general.

Restoring Trust in American Business, the first publication of the American Academy's Corporate Responsibility project, brings together leading scholars and practitioners with diverse views to reflect more broadly on how the collapse occurred and suggest productive strategies for change. The American business community must do more to restore badly eroded investor and public trust. The legislative and regulatory response to date, as well as the bulk of commentary, has focused on the relationships among senior managers, the board of directors, and shareholders; on accounting and audit practice; on executive compensation; and on rules regarding the board, its composition, and its relationship with the firm's auditors.

To be sure, the principal responsibility for corporate misconduct, when it occurs, rests with corporate management and boards of directors; and the restoration of trust in American business will require of CEOs and boards an increased commitment to the larger society and to the stewardship of the corporate institution. However, recent governance failures are not limited to management and boards. They extend well beyond the boundaries of the corporation, suggesting that the supporting institutions outside the boardroom also need attention. This report focuses on how these supporting institutions can play a more constructive role in shaping corporate conduct.

THE FAILURE OF THE *GATEKEEPERS*

The American market-oriented system relies primarily on marketplace actors and private gatekeepers to check and warranty corporate conduct. Certainly, governmental regulators (including quasi-public, self-regulatory organizations with regulatory roles, such as the stock exchanges) deter and punish corporate wrongdoing with the "stick" of rule enforcement; and better rules or stronger enforcement might have prevented more of the corporate malfeasance. But the regulatory stick is a blunt instrument. Moreover, our political process renders regulatory agencies vulnerable to private actors' efforts to diminish their funding and weaken their oversight capabilities.

Clearly, the regulators did not prevent the recent wave of corporate malfeasance; nor did companies' boards of directors; nor did their auditors, lawyers and investment bankers; nor did the business press. Each group had some opportunity—and some, an explicit professional obligation—to constrain corporate management, and to safeguard the public's trust in business and in our capitalist system. Yet each of these groups got caught up in powerful market pressures that undermined their commitment to "doing the right thing," whether for clients, the general public, or both. The failure was exceptionally pronounced during the long-running bull market of the 1990s. During that time, a culture of greed compromised professionalism and produced rampant conflicts of interest on the part of professional service providers.

For more than a century, an invaluable centerpiece of the American economy has been our large public securities markets, through which the public directly and indirectly invests its capital in corporations. In spite of occasional failures, these capital markets have been perceived, both by U.S. investors and by individuals and governments around the world, as basically transparent and honest. These markets constitute important national assets. The businesses that have been financed through them have brought the benefits of science and technology to consumers throughout the world, raising the American—and the global—standard of living. But this success story was not inevitable; it has depended upon an infrastructure of law, regulation and enforcement, and on a network of supporting institutions that promote public trust.

Among the most important of these supporting institutions are those we refer to in this volume as the *gatekeepers*. These *gatekeepers* include lawyers, accountants and journalists, as well as corporate directors, regulators and investment bankers. While these occupations are not all viewed as full-fledged professions, each performs a vital function in facilitating the production of wealth in a fair and efficient way.[1] What all of these *gatekeeper* groups have in common is that the public expects them to discharge their responsibilities with integrity, and—more explicitly in the case of the recognized professions—to foster the public good. The failure of this network of *gatekeepers* was a recurring theme in the business scandals. In too many instances, the *gatekeepers* in pursuit of their own financial self-interest compromised the values and standards of their professions. Had managers always acted with integrity, the *gatekeepers'* failures would not have been so costly. The *gatekeepers* are expected to constrain the primary corporate actors—America's managers—from acting badly. In the most recent round of corporate scandals, the first tier—the managers—failed; and then the *gatekeepers* failed as well.

[1] The essay in this volume titled "Management as a Profession" enumerates several criteria that collectively define a "profession." These include a common body of knowledge, member certification and licensing, a code of ethics and sanctioning mechanism, and an explicit commitment to the public good.

It is now apparent that there has been a systematic decline in the status and role of America's professions, including those to which business firms have traditionally looked for counsel and judgment. In the intensely market-driven economy of the 1980s and 1990s, many professionals ceased to be trusted advisors and sound counselors, capable of appropriately mediating among the short-run and long-term interests of business firms and the larger interests of society. Instead, they came to view their role as simply advancing management's interests. The result is the troubling number of professional advisors who failed to do their part in preventing the corporate scandals. The number and magnitude of corporate wrongdoing cases would have been almost inconceivable had these professionals behaved consistently with their traditional roles and the public's legitimate expectations.

REBUILDING PROFESSIONALISM FOR THE TWENTY-FIRST CENTURY

As a society, we face the challenge of rebuilding professional standards in a world of interdependent markets that are more global and more powerful than ever before. These markets have grown to the point where they dominate the structures that were invented, in another era, to channel their energies productively. Market participants have also changed radically; investors have become global, larger, more diverse in their goals, and more anonymous than ever before.

In this enormously complex and fluid environment, responsible corporate conduct depends on public spirited *gatekeepers* exercising independent professional judgment. *Gatekeepers* cannot perform their vital functions if they are reduced to mere facilitators of management or captives of short-term market forces.

It is time to reimagine and rebuild these *gatekeeper* roles in order to empower them to more constructively shape corporate conduct. It is also time to give more serious thought to the scope of the public obligations of corporate management beyond simple compliance with the law.

The recommendations that follow emerge from a series of workshops and discussions convened by the American Academy's Corporate Responsibility project. We begin with several recommendations for stronger boards of directors, but focus as well on the other *gatekeeper* roles. We have also included some thoughts on institutional shareholders, and the need for ongoing professional education. The recommendations propose a direction for action, and also represent an effort to stimulate further conversation. What is more important than any specific recommendation is the realization that the challenge of restoring trust in American business will continue to require the urgent attention and cooperative efforts of our nation's intellectual, business, and public leaders.

Recommendations
for Practice

RECOMMENDATIONS FOR DIRECTORS

■ **Oversight Role.** In recent years there have been a number
of high-profile failures of public company boards. Some
Committee members see these failures as exceptions within a
broader pattern of improved board performance over the past
decade, while others point to data on misleading financial
reporting and excessive executive compensation as evidence,
among other things, that these failures arise out of a general
culture of board passivity. Committee members agree, however,
that the standard of performance in American boardrooms must
be raised. Moreover, the debate sparked by recent high-profile
failures points to the need to clarify the role of boards in public
corporations. The primary role that the American corporate
governance system has assigned to the board is to set and oversee the company's direction, and to appoint, oversee, compensate and, where appropriate, replace management. The board
also gives advice and makes several important kinds of decisions,
including approving the company's strategy. The board has ultimate legal responsibility for the company, and is the primary
"gatekeeper" for ensuring that operating managers act with
integrity and competence. But it cannot as a practical matter, and
should not, attempt to run the company on a day-to-day basis;
it must delegate this responsibility to management. The board is
responsible for having monitoring systems in place to help
ensure that the firm is running well.

■ **Corporate Ethics.** Directors have oversight responsibility for
the legal and ethical conduct of the corporation. Boards must
therefore ensure that companies have appropriate ethics policies
and compliance systems. On a day-to-day basis, however, a com-

pany's ethical tone is set by top management, and in particular the CEO. Boards must therefore give as much consideration to the integrity and ethical standards of CEOs (and CEO candidates) and other senior management as to their business competence.

■ **Professional Standards.** Although corporate directors are not now usually viewed as comprising a "profession," the members of the director community should bring a spirit of professionalism to their responsibilities. Directors should view themselves as trustees of the interests of shareholders and the corporation. For most companies, these interests will properly be construed as the shareholders' and the corporate institution's *long-term* interests, although there are also circumstances in which directors are obligated to consider more short-term interests as well. In order to fulfill their obligations, board members must devote sufficient time and effort to performing their duties, including being adequately informed about the company's affairs.

■ **Independent Leadership.** The Committee endorses the continuing trend in favor of boards composed of a majority of directors who are independent of management and have no material interests which conflict with their responsibilities as directors. The independent directors' effectiveness is greatly enhanced by having a leader who is also independent of management. It is appropriate for each board to determine, in light of all relevant circumstances, whether that independent leadership is best provided by a non-executive chairman of the board, or by designating and empowering a "lead" or "presiding" director. Regardless of the chosen structure, the independent directors should meet on a regular basis without management.

■ **Executive Compensation.** Boards and their compensation committees should structure the CEO's compensation to reflect the shareholders' and corporation's long-term interests. In setting the compensation of top executives, directors must take into account employment market conditions and the need to motivate and retain talented individuals, as well as what is acceptable to shareholders. But they should also be mindful of the corporate sector's collective interest in maintaining public support and confidence in business, and the impact that extravagant compensation terms—particularly terms that do not seem to correlate well with performance—have had on undermining that support and confidence. A set of "best practice" principles that would better tie compensation to long-term performance would be welcome.

■ **Shareholder Input in Director Nominations.** The Committee acknowledges a diversity of opinion among its members regarding the merits of the "shareholder access" proposed rule issued by the Securities and Exchange Commission. This proposed rule would permit shareholders meeting certain criteria, including certain triggering events, to nominate a "short slate" of director candidates directly on the company's proxy materials. Some members of the Committee support this proposed rule and others oppose it. However the SEC ultimately rules on this matter, the Committee agrees that the nominating/corporate governance committees responsible for nominating candidates for election to the board should be attentive to shareholders' concerns and preferences regarding nominees.

■ **Auditor Oversight and "Fair Presentation."** The Committee applauds the assignment of the auditor oversight role under the Sarbanes-Oxley Act to the board via its audit committee. In performing this oversight role, audit committees should explicitly acknowledge that the "fair presentation" standard applicable to companies' financial disclosure goes beyond mere compliance with GAAP rules, and that it requires that the company provide a transparent view of its financial results and condition.

RECOMMENDATIONS FOR INSTITUTIONAL SHAREHOLDERS

■ **Governance Responsibilities**. Institutional investors, and the firms that manage their funds, should acknowledge their duty to ensure that companies in their portfolios adopt good governance practices. They should also acknowledge their duty to actively review and vote upon proxy resolutions. To meet this objective, institutional investors should make reasoned, independent decisions on proxy votes. They should neither mechanically support company managements' positions, nor automatically follow the recommendations of proxy advisory services. While they may appropriately rely on expert advice in this area as in other areas, institutions should recognize that proxy voting is a fiduciary responsibility that ultimately lies with the institutional investor itself, and not with the advisor. Further, company managements and boards should be encouraged to focus on long-term strategic goals while also managing short-term market pressures.

■ **Governance Standards.** Institutional investors and investment management companies should adopt their own vigorous governance standards, adhering to their own fiduciary duties to those who invest money with them. As fiduciaries, institutional investors and investment management companies should scrupulously refrain from activities that subordinate the interests of their investors to other objectives.

RECOMMENDATIONS FOR REGULATORS

■ **General Standards of Conduct.** Leaders of regulatory, self-regulatory and judicial bodies (including the Chairs of the Securities and Exchange Commission (SEC), the Public Company Accounting Oversight Board (PCAOB), and the National Association of Securities Dealers (NASD); the leaders of the stock exchanges; and the members of the Delaware court, among others) should actively use their "bully pulpits" to encourage the highest standards of conduct for corporate management, boards of directors, professional advisors, and those affiliated with their organizations.

■ **SEC Independence.** Congress must fully respect the SEC's status as an independent agency, and commit to funding levels for it that are adequate for the vigorous enforcement of laws and regulations. The SEC should vigilantly guard its independence against short-term political and budgetary pressures. Corporations and their lobbyists must refrain from seeking to starve the SEC of funding in the pursuit of their own narrow policy objectives.

■ **Investor Education.** The SEC Chair, among others, should speak publicly and aggressively to encourage managers and institutional shareholders, as well as other investors, to carefully attend to issues of disclosure, fiduciary responsibility and conflicts of interest that affect the value of their shares. Effective managerial, institutional, and investor education should be a priority of the SEC, along with enforcement, inspection and disclosure review.

■ **Stock Exchanges.** The stock exchanges should institute vigorous governance standards of their own, in light of their role in setting and monitoring the governance standards of listed companies. They should further consider what additional role they can play in fostering high quality, cost-effective corporate governance in listed firms.

RECOMMENDATIONS FOR LAWYERS

■ **Professional Standards.** The legal profession as a whole, as well as individual law firms, must reflect thoughtfully and critically on why some members of the profession have strayed from the highest standards of professionalism. The failure of lawyers to prevent corporate misconduct suggests that they can become beholden to corporate management. Lawyers representing companies must understand that, while the corporate entity acts through its management, the ultimate "client" is the corporation. Lawyers must bear in mind their responsibilities to that ultimate client, even as they properly take direction from members of management. Moreover, beyond the duty business lawyers owe to the client, lawyers owe a further professional duty to represent the client in a manner that is consistent with the public values elaborated below. Law firms must develop cultures that inculcate these duties in their members.

■ **Business Lawyers' Duty of Independence**. The Committee urges leaders of the legal profession, as well as legal educators, to emphasize the need for business lawyers to act as *independent* legal counsel. The conception of lawyers as "zealous advocates" has long dominated the profession. This conception—which authorizes lawyers to adopt on their client's behalf every advantageous construction of law that is not plainly erroneous—has social utility in the litigation context, where positions are tested by an informed adversary and evaluated by an expert and disinterested judge. But in the context of facilitating business transactions, where these judicial safeguards are initially absent, commitment to facilitating every advantageous transaction, unless no technically possible interpretation of the law can be found to support it, can lead to socially destructive action. Leadership of the legal profession should endorse, and include in statements of the professional obligations of business lawyers, the principle that such lawyers owe a public duty to the law itself, in addition to the loyalty and confidentiality that they owe to their clients. That public duty can be expressed as a duty to the discernible spirit that animates the positive law.

■ **"Up-the-Ladder" Reporting Obligation.** We applaud the SEC's attorney professional conduct rule that requires lawyers to report a client's material legal non-compliance, when they become aware of it in the course of a representation, "up the ladder" to the client corporation's board of directors, if necessary; and that the lawyers withdraw from further representation of the client if the board fails to take timely steps to remedy the non-compliance.

■ **Lawyer Withdrawal Reporting Obligation.** The Committee acknowledges a diversity of opinion among its members regarding the merits of the "noisy withdrawal" proposed rule issued by the Securities and Exchange Commission. This proposed rule would require lawyers to report their withdrawal to the SEC, an obligation that would be in tension with the lawyer-client privilege. Some Committee members favor this "noisy withdrawal" obligation, while others do not. Even those Committee members opposed to a "noisy withdrawal" obligation agree that, at a minimum, the SEC should require the client company to report the lawyers' withdrawal to the SEC, except where a committee of independent directors advised by independent counsel has determined that the withdrawing lawyers had not acted reasonably.

■ **Lawyer Independence and Compensation.** Lawyers and law firms must ensure that their fee arrangements with clients do not compromise their capacity to fulfill their duty of independence, and to conform to the highest professional standards. Various types of current fee arrangements have the potential for creating conflicts of interest or otherwise for impairing lawyer independence. Law firms should carefully scrutinize their policies concerning fee arrangements with clients to ensure that independence and professional standards are in no way compromised.

RECOMMENDATIONS FOR AUDITORS

■ **Professional Standards.** The accounting profession must return to the high standards of professionalism it had in an earlier era, and must search for the reasons for its decline. Auditors play an indispensable role in regard to transparent financial reporting. The complicity of accounting professionals in cases of fraudulent or misleading financial reporting suggests that auditors, in some cases, failed to maintain appropriate independence from corporate management. The accounting profession must now fully embrace the legislative mandate that it is the board of directors—and its audit committee—that is the auditor's "client." Moreover, auditors of public companies owe a further professional duty to the investing public. The extreme concentration of public company auditors in a small number of firms may itself be problematic. Particularly in light of that concentration, it is critically important that each of these firms develops standards and a culture that serve to inculcate these obligations in its professionals.

■ **The Auditor Role.** The Committee endorses the mandate that accounting firms refocus on the audit function (while recognizing that many corporate clients continue to engage them for tax work as well). There remains, however, a need to clarify more precisely the scope of the audit function in regard to corporate misconduct risk and corporate business risk. This clarification will help to ensure that auditors are fully accountable for the function they undertake, but not subjected to unreasonable expectations beyond that function.

■ **"Fair Presentation."** Auditors should embrace their responsibilities for the "fair presentation" of a company's financial condition and results of operations; and should explicitly acknowledge that their responsibilities under this standard go beyond compliance with GAAP rules.

■ **Principles-Based Accounting.** The accounting profession is urged to move even further in the direction of a principles-based accounting regime, in order to minimize the opportunity for company financial disclosure that technically complies with rules while misleading the investing public. Bright lines are both constraints and safe harbors for companies and auditors. A move away from rules toward a principles-based system will, on the one hand, give companies and auditors greater flexibility in accurately portraying firms' economic position; but, on the other hand, it will necessarily subject companies and auditors to greater scrutiny as to whether they did, in fact, accomplish this goal. While this move should benefit all concerned, it will require careful and thoughtful oversight by both the Financial Accounting Standards Boards and the Public Company Accounting Oversight Board.

RECOMMENDATIONS FOR INVESTMENT BANKERS

■ **Professional Standards.** Investment banking has been transformed in recent decades. The traditional role of the investment banker as a company's long-term, "senior advisor" has become overwhelmed by a more transaction-based business. Unlike law or accounting, investment banking is not viewed presently as a "profession." It is, however, composed of highly skilled and well-compensated practitioners who (among other things) advise clients about major decisions that impact the investing public. More broadly, investment banking has become an important sector of the economy, both as a stand-alone industry and in terms of its great influence on the corporate sector. Investment bankers engaged by companies must understand that, while the corporate entity acts through its management, the ultimate "client" is the corporation. Investment bankers also must bear in mind their responsibilities to that ultimate client, even as they properly take direction from members of management. Moreover, in addition to the duty they owe to the client, investment banking firms should reflect on the nature of the obligations they may owe to the larger investing public in the performance of their various functions, beyond complying with the law. They should collaborate to establish a uniform code of conduct that articulates their obligations to clients and to the investing public. They should also establish formal training modules to teach appropriate guidelines and conduct to their professional staff. These steps toward professionalization could serve as a model for other sectors in the financial services industry that have been similarly transformed in recent decades (including, without limitation, the mutual funds and commercial banking businesses).

■ **Managing Conflicts of Interest.** The investment banking industry has been prone to conflicts of interest, partly reflecting its broad range of interrelated service offerings. These include the well-documented conflict between securities underwriting and investment research, as well as the potential for conflict between investment banking and commercial lending activities.

Independently of any regulatory initiatives in this area, investment banks should reflect carefully on the potential for conflicts created by their multiple businesses. They should disclose, to clients and to the public, these potential conflicts and the policies in place for managing them. A key priority should be to ensure that equity analysts perform and report independent, unbiased, and non-self-serving assessments of the companies they follow; and to ensure the economic viability of independent equity research.

RECOMMENDATIONS FOR JOURNALISTS

■ **Business Reporting Mission and Professional Standards.** The press is expected to play a critically important "watchdog" and informational role in a democracy, a role that extends to the world of business. Media firms must clarify and publicly articulate their mission regarding business reporting and develop appropriate standards of professionalism and codes of conduct for journalists who cover business. These missions and standards should include a commitment to traditional "Fourth Estate" values—including independence and objectivity—which should never be compromised by media firms' own profit pressures.

■ **Greater Objectivity.** Journalists have a professional and public duty to report objectively and accurately on business. Business desk editors and individual journalists should be wary of the risk of losing objectivity and getting caught up in current emotions. It appears that this tendency has caused some journalists to "cheerlead" during bull markets, and to presume corporate guilt in the post-scandal environment. Outside the editorial pages, business journalists must be scrupulously independent and objective. They should bring open minds to the stories they cover and strive for the greatest possible accuracy in their factual reporting.

■ **Legislator Conflicts of Interest.** The press can make an important contribution to the functioning of the corporate governance system by increasing transparency where relationships are otherwise opaque. In that regard, the Committee urges that, in the course of covering pending legislation, the press systematically disclose legislators' conflicts of interests where they have received campaign contributions from parties whose interests are directly affected. Moreover, the press should be alert to how private actors in our market economy can influence the legislature to reduce the funding of those responsible for regulating those private actors.

RECOMMENDATIONS FOR PROFESSIONAL AND CONTINUING EDUCATION

■ **Professional Education**. The "teaching" of ethical conduct should take place at every level of education, as well as within each profession and each firm. Within this broader context, professional schools play a key role. Beyond a single course in ethics, professional schools should consider incorporating ethical standards modules throughout the curriculum, which should include case studies that highlight both ethical and unethical conduct. Among other things, they should examine how business structures can provide incentives (and eliminate disincentives) for managers to act ethically. Professional schools should closely examine their curricula in this regard. The various professions should also develop appropriate ethics curricula for the continuing education of their members.

■ **Education Within the Firm.** The leadership of individual firms should also take steps to ensure that the firm has a culture of ethical conduct, and to mitigate against the explicit and implicit pressures for better performance that can undercut ethical standards. The ethical standards of the firm should be explicitly discussed and taught to professional staff *in situ*, in addition to the ethics training received outside the firm. These efforts are particularly important in regard to the emerging professions.

About the Co-Chairs

MARTIN LIPTON, a founding partner of Wachtell, Lipton, Rosen & Katz, specializes in advising major corporations on mergers and acquisitions and matters affecting corporate policy and strategy, and has written and lectured extensively on these subjects. Mr. Lipton is Chairman of The Board of Trustees of New York University, a Trustee of the New York University School of Law (Chairman 1988–1998), a member of the Council of the American Law Institute, Co-Chair of the Partnership for New York City, and a Director of the Institute of Judicial Administration. Mr. Lipton served as Special Counsel to the City of New York in connection with the fiscal crisis (1975–1978); Special Counsel, United States Department of Energy (1979–1980); and Acting General Counsel, United States Synthetic Fuels Corporation (1980). Mr. Lipton served as counsel to the New York Stock Exchange Committee on Market Structure, Governance and Ownership (1999–2000), as counsel to, and member of, its Committee on Corporate Accountability and Listing Standards [Corporate Governance] (2002) and as Chairman of its Legal Advisory Committee (2002–2004). Mr. Lipton has a B.S. in Economics from the Wharton School of the University of Pennsylvania and an L.L.B. from the New York University School of Law. He is a Fellow of the American Academy of Arts and Sciences.

JAY W. LORSCH is the Louis Kirstein Professor of Human Relations at the Harvard Business School. He is the author of over a dozen books, including *Back to the Drawing Board: Designing Corporate Boards for a Complex World* (2003), *Aligning The Stars: How to Succeed When Professionals Drive Results* (2002), and *Pawns or Potentates: The Reality of America's Corporate Boards* (1989). *Organization and Environment* (with Paul R. Lawrence) won the Academy of Management's Best Management Book of the Year Award (1967). Having taught in all of Harvard Business School's educational programs, he was Chairman of Doctoral Programs,

Senior Associate Dean and Chair of the Executive Education Programs, 1991–1995; Senior Associate Dean and Director of Research, 1986–1991; Chairman of the Advanced Management Program, 1980–1985; and prior to that was Chairman of the Organizational Behavior Area. Professor Lorsch is a Director of Blasland, Bouck & Lee, Inc. and Computer Associates, and a member of the Advisory Board of U.S. Foodservice and BoardVantage, Inc. He is a graduate of Antioch College (1955) with an M.S. degree in Business from Columbia University (1956) and a Doctor of Business Administration from Harvard Business School (1964). At Columbia, he was a Samuel Bronfman Fellow in Democratic Business Administration. From 1956–1959, he served as a Lieutenant in the U.S. Army Finance Corp.

LARRY SONSINI is the chairman and chief executive officer of the law firm of Wilson Sonsini Goodrich & Rosati, where he specializes in corporate law, corporate governance, securities, and mergers and acquisitions. He holds an A.B. from the University of California at Berkeley, and a J.D. from Boalt Hall School of Law, where he has been a faculty member since 1985. He is a Fellow of the American Academy of Arts and Sciences, a member of the American Law Institute, a trustee of Santa Clara University, a member of the University of California President's Board on Science and Innovation, and a former trustee of UC Berkeley. Mr. Sonsini is currently Chairman of the New York Stock Exchange's Regulation, Enforcement and Listing Standards Committee, and Chairman of the NYSE Legal Advisory Committee. He served on the Board of Directors of the NYSE from 2001 to 2003, during which time he was also a member of the NYSE's Corporate Accountability and Listing Standards Committee and the NYSE/NASD IPO Advisory Committee. He has also served on the SEC's Advisory Committee on Capital Formation and Regulatory Processes; the ABA Committee on Federal Regulation of Securities; and the Legal Advisory Board of the NASD, Inc. Mr. Sonsini is a director of the following public companies: Brocade Communications Systems, Inc., Echelon Corporation, LSI Logic Corporation, PIXAR, Inc. and Silicon Valley Bancshares.

About the Authors

WILLIAM T. ALLEN is the Jack Nusbaum Professor of Law & Business at New York University and the Director of the NYU Center for Law & Business. From 1985 until 1997 he served as Chancellor of the Court of Chancery of the State of Delaware. In that position he wrote numerous judicial opinions concerning the fiduciary obligations of corporate officers and directors. Professor Allen serves as counsel to the New York law firm Wachtell, Lipton, Rosen & Katz. Among other affiliations, he is a member of the American Law Institute and a Fellow of the American Academy of Arts and Sciences.

LESLIE BERLOWITZ is the Executive Officer of the American Academy of Arts and Sciences, a 223-year-old international learned society headquartered in Cambridge, Massachusetts. She is the first woman to serve in this post. Prior to coming to the Academy, she served as Vice President for Academic Advancement at New York University. Her training is in American Literature, and she has co-edited *America in Theory* with Denis Donoghue and Louis Menand, and *Greenwich Village: Culture and Counterculture* with Richard Eric Beard. Ms. Berlowitz serves on the boards of a number of national non-profit organizations. She was educated at New York University and Columbia University. Ms. Berlowitz is a Fellow of the American Academy of Arts and Sciences.

JOHN H. BIGGS is former Chairman, President, and Chief Executive Officer of TIAA-CREF. He holds an A.B. degree in classics from Harvard University, and a Ph.D. in economics from Washington University, St. Louis. Mr. Biggs is a Director of the Boeing Company and JPMorgan Chase Co., and a Trustee of the International Accounting Standards Committee Foundation, Washington University, The Danforth Foundation in St. Louis, The Santa Fe Opera, the J. Paul Getty Trust (Chairman) and Emeriti. He is also a Director and former Chairman of the United Way of

New York City and the National Bureau of Economic Research, and a Fellow of the American Academy of Arts and Sciences.

MARGARET M. BLAIR is a Professor of Law at Vanderbilt University Law School. She holds a B.A. from the University of Oklahoma and an M.A., M.Phil., and Ph.D. in economics from Yale University. She recently moved to Vanderbilt from Georgetown University Law Center, where she was a Sloan Visiting Professor, teaching Corporations and Corporate Finance, and Research Director for the Sloan-GULC Project on Business Institutions. Professor Blair has also been a Senior Fellow in the Economic Studies Program at the Brookings Institution. Her current research is on team production and the legal structure of business organizations, on trust as a mechanism of governance in business firms, and on the culture of boards of directors.

RAKESH KHURANA is an associate professor of organizational behavior at Harvard Business School. His research interests are executive labor markets, especially the processes by which leaders are identified, sorted, and selected. Khurana has published several articles, cases, and book chapters on the subject and is also the author of *Searching for a Corporate Savior: The Irrational Quest for Charismatic CEOs* (Princeton University Press, 2002). Currently he is working on a project examining the social transformation of American business education and the process by which leaders create meaning for those working in organizations.

WILLIAM R. KINNEY, JR. holds a Ph.D. from Michigan State University. He has taught accounting and auditing at Iowa, Michigan, INSEAD, and now Texas, where he holds the Prothro Chair in Business. He has written more than 50 articles in refereed scholarly accounting journals. Recently, his research has addressed earnings management, stock price reaction to earnings surprise, and the relation of audit firm fees to financial restatements. Professor Kinney's service includes editorship of the *Accounting Review,* and memberships on the AICPA's Auditing Standards Board and the FASB's Financial Accounting Advisory Council. He has twice received the Wildman Award and the Notable Contribution to the Accounting Literature Award.

MICHAEL KLAUSNER is the Nancy and Charles Munger Professor of Business and Professor of Law at Stanford Law School, where he teaches and writes on corporate law and corporate governance. His writing includes theoretical and empirical articles on corporate governance. He graduated in 1981 from Yale University with a J.D. and an M.A. in economics, and clerked for Judge David Bazelon and Justice William Brennan. He was in private practice from 1985 to 1989 and then served as a White House Fellow in the Office of Policy Development at the White House. Prior to joining the Stanford faculty, he was on the faculty at New York University.

DONALD C. LANGEVOORT is the Thomas Aquinas Reynolds Professor of Law at Georgetown University Law Center, Washington, D.C. He joined the Georgetown faculty in 1999 after eighteen years at Vanderbilt University School of Law, where he had been the Lee S. & Charles A. Speir Professor. He has also been a visiting professor at the University of Michigan, Harvard Law School, and the University of Sydney in Australia. After graduating from Harvard Law School, he worked at the law firm of Wilmer, Cutler & Pickering, and in the Office of the General Counsel of the U.S. Securities & Exchange Commission. Professor Langevoort has published extensively on securities regulation and investor behavior. He is a member of the American Law Institute.

GEOFFREY MILLER is the Stuyvesant P. and William T. III Comfort Professor of Law at New York University Law School and Director of its Center for the Study of Central Banks. After graduating from Columbia University Law School, where he was Editor-in-Chief of the Law Review, he clerked for Judge Carl McGowan and Justice Byron White, and worked at the United States Department of Justice and a private law firm. Prior to joining NYU, Professor Miller was the Kirkland & Ellis Professor at the University of Chicago Law School. He is the author of three books and more than one hundred scholarly articles in the fields of corporate law, banking law, legal ethics, separation of powers, civil procedure, and law and economics.

NITIN NOHRIA is Richard P. Chapman Professor of Business Administration at the Harvard Business School. His teaching and research centers on leadership, corporate accountability, and organizational change. Co-author of ten books, his most recent include: *What Really Works: The 4+2 Formula for Sustained Business Success* (HarperCollins, 2003), a systematic large-scale study of management practices that create business winners; *Changing Fortunes: Remaking the Industrial Corporation* (John Wiley & Sons, 2002), which examines the decline of industrial firms in the late twentieth century and discusses lessons from this experience; and *Driven: How Human Nature Shapes our Choices* (Jossey-Bass, 2002), which explores four basic drives underlying human motivation. He is also the author of over 75 journal articles, book chapters, and teaching cases.

GENEVA OVERHOLSER holds the Hurley Chair in Public Affairs Reporting in the Missouri School of Journalism's Washington bureau and writes a weblog at www.poynter.org. She is former editor of the *Des Moines Register*, which won a Pulitzer Prize for Public Service under her leadership. She is a former ombudsman of the *Washington Post* and editorial board member of the *New York Times*. She is a fellow of the Society of Professional Journalists, and a former officer of the American Society of Newspaper Editors, Nieman fellow, and member and chair of the Pulitzer Prize Board. She is a Fellow of the American Academy of Arts and Sciences.

RICHARD W. PAINTER is the Guy Raymond and Mildred Van Voorhis Jones Professor at the University of Illinois College of Law. He holds an A.B. from Harvard University and a J.D. from Yale University. He clerked for the Hon. John T. Noonan, Jr., and was associated with Sullivan & Cromwell and Finn Dixon & Herling. Professor Painter is the author of numerous publications, including a casebook on securities litigation and two editions of a casebook on legal ethics (with Judge Noonan). A key provision of the Sarbanes-Oxley Act of 2002, requiring the SEC to issue rules of professional responsibility for securities lawyers, was based on earlier proposals Professor Painter had made in law review articles.

DANIEL PENRICE is a research associate at the Harvard Business School. He has worked as a writer and editor for management consulting firms and written for management publications including *Harvard Business Review*. As an HBS research associate, he worked with Rakesh Khurana on *Searching for a Corporate Savior: The Irrational Quest for Charismatic CEOs* (Princeton University Press, 2002).

JOHN S. REED is a Fellow and Treasurer of the American Academy of Arts and Sciences. He serves as Chair of the New York Stock Exchange. Mr. Reed retired in 2000 as chair and chief executive officer of Citigroup Inc., a company founded by the merger of Citicorp and Travelers Group in 1998. In his thirty-five-year career, he was also chairman and chief executive officer of Citigroup's subsidiaries, Citicorp and Citibank. Mr. Reed serves on the boards of the Center for Advanced Study in the Behavioral Sciences in Palo Alto, the Spencer Foundation in Chicago, and the RAND Corporation. He is also a member of the American Philosophical Society, the MIT Corporation, and the board of Altria Group, Inc.

MARK J. ROE is the David Berg Professor of Corporate Law at Harvard Law School, where he teaches bankruptcy and corporate law. His publications include *Political Determinants of Corporate Governance* (Oxford University Press, 2003); *Strong Managers, Weak Owners* (Princeton University Press, 1994); "The Institutions of Corporate Governance," in the *Handbook of Institutional Economics* (forthcoming, 2005); "Corporate Law's Limits," *Journal of Legal Studies* 31 (2002): 233; and "Delaware's Competition," *Harvard Law Review* 117 (2003): 588.

FELIX G. ROHATYN is President of Rohatyn Associates LLC in New York. He served as U.S. Ambassador to France from 1997 to 2000. Prior to that, he was managing director of the investment banking firm Lazard Frères & Co. LLC, in New York, where he had worked for nearly 50 years. Ambassador Rohatyn also served as Chairman of the Municipal Assistance Corporation (MAC) of the State of New York, where he managed negotiations that enabled New York City to solve its financial crisis in the 1970s. He has served as a member of the Board of Governors of the New York

Stock Exchange and as a director of a number of American and French corporations. He is a Fellow of the American Academy of Arts and Sciences.

GERALD ROSENFELD is Chief Executive Officer of Rothschild North America. Prior to joining Rothschild, he was President of G Rosenfeld & Co. LLC, an investment banking firm. Prior to founding GR & Co. in 1998, he was Head of Investment Banking and a member of the Management Committee of Lazard Frères & Co. LLC. Mr. Rosenfeld is a member of the Board of Directors of Resources Connection and ContiGroup Companies, and also serves on the Board of Overseers of New York University's Stern School of Business. He holds a Ph.D. in Applied Mathematics from New York University and is an Adjunct Professor of Finance at the New York University Stern School of Business. He is a Fellow of the American Academy of Arts and Sciences.

DAMON SILVERS is an Associate General Counsel for the AFL-CIO. He led the AFL-CIO legal team that won severance payments for laid-off Enron and WorldCom workers. He is a member of the Public Company Accounting Oversight Board Standing Advisory Group, and the Financial Accounting Standards Board User Advisory Council. Mr. Silvers is the primary author of "Challenging Wall Street's Conventional Wisdom: Defining a Worker-Owner View of Value," published in Fung et al., eds., *Working Capital: The Power of Labor's Pensions* (Cornell University Press, 2001), and "The Origins and Goals of the Fight for Proxy Access," in Lucian Bebchuk, ed., *Shareholder Access to the Corporate Ballot* (Harvard University Press, 2004).

ANDY ZELLEKE is the project director of the American Academy's Corporate Responsibility study. He is a lecturer in the Legal Studies Department at the University of Pennsylvania's Wharton School, where he teaches negotiation. He has previously been a lecturer at the UCLA School of Law. Dr. Zelleke's research focuses on boards of directors, the design of governance and leadership structures, and comparative corporate governance. He holds an A.B. and a Ph.D. from Harvard University, and a J.D. from Harvard Law School.

THE AMERICAN ACADEMY OF ARTS & SCIENCES

Founded in 1780, the American Academy of Arts and Sciences is an international learned society composed of the world's leading scientists, scholars, artists, business people, and public leaders. With a current membership of 3,700 American Fellows and 600 Foreign Honorary Members, the Academy has four major goals:

- Promoting service and study through analysis of critical social and intellectual issues and the development of practical policy alternatives;

- Fostering public engagement and the exchange of ideas with meetings, conferences, and symposia bringing diverse perspectives to the examination of issues of common concern;

- Mentoring a new generation of scholars and thinkers through its Visiting Scholars Program;

- Honoring excellence by electing to membership men and women in a broad range of disciplines and professions.

The Academy's main headquarters are in Cambridge, Massachusetts.

OFFICERS OF THE AMERICAN ACADEMY